The Arab-African Connection

Other Westview Special Studies on Africa

Apartheid and International Organizations, Richard E. Bissell

Ethnicity in Modern Africa, edited by Brian M. du Toit

Zambia's Foreign Policy: Studies in Diplomacy and Dependence, Douglas G. Anglin and Timothy M. Shaw

Botswana: An African Growth Economy, Penelope Hartland-Thunberg

South Africa Into the 1980s, edited by Richard E. Bissell and Chester A. Crocker

Crisis in Zimbabwe, edited by Boniface I. Obichere

Other Westview Special Studies on the Middle East

Oil, the Arab-Israel Dispute, and the Industrial World: Horizons of Crisis, edited by J. C. Hurewitz

The Persian Gulf: An Introduction to Its People, Politics, and Economics, David E. Long

The Middle East: Critical Choices for the United States, edited by Eugene V. Rostow

Yemen: The Politics of the Yemen Arab Republic, Robert W. Stookey

Armed Struggle in Palestine: An Analysis of the Palestinian Guerrilla Movement, Bard O'Neill

The Modern Middle East: A Guide to Research Tools in the Social Sciences, Reeva S. Simon

The United Arab Emirates, Ali Mohammed Khalifa

Economic Growth and Development in Jordan, Michael P. Mazur

Westview Special Studies on Africa/The Middle East

The Arab-African Connection:
Political and Economic Realities
Victor T. Le Vine and Timothy W. Luke

Between June 1967 and the end of 1973, most independent Black African states abandoned their neutral position in the Middle East conflict, cut their ties with Israel, and gave full support to the political aims of the Arab states. Since the beginning of 1974, however, and despite attempts by the Arabs to shield their new allies from the adverse effects of the 1973-74 world oil and economic crises, the alliance has begun to fragment as the African states become transformed from partners to clients and dependents of the Arabs.

This study examines the roots of the African conversion, the nature of the evolving relationship between the African and Arab states, and the reasons—economic and political—for the transformation of the alliance. Basic to that transformation, the authors argue, is a fundamental change in the international status and power of the Arab states, a change that has led them to cast their lot with the industrialized "First World" rather than with the poorer, less developed countries.

Victor T. Le Vine is professor of political science at Washington University and was previously professor and head, Department of Political Science, University of Ghana. Timothy W. Luke is a teaching fellow in political science at Washington University.

The Arab-African Connection:
Political and Economic Realities

Victor T. Le Vine
and Timothy W. Luke

Westview Press / Boulder, Colorado

Westview Special Studies on Africa/The Middle East

Copyright © 1979 by Westview Press, Inc.

Published in 1979 in the United States of America by
  Westview Press, Inc.
  5500 Central Avenue
  Boulder, Colorado 80301
  Frederick A. Praeger, Publisher

Library of Congress Cataloging in Publication Data
Le Vine, Victor T.
  The Arab-African connection.
  (A Westview special study)
  1. Arab countries—Foreign relations—Africa. 2. Africa—Foreign relations—Arab countries. 3. Arab countries—Foreign economic relations—Africa. 4. Africa—Foreign economic relations—Arab countries. I. Luke, Timothy W., joint author. II. Title.
DS63.2.A4L48   327.6'017-7'4927   78-27362
ISBN 0-89158-398-X

Printed and bound in the United States of America

Contents

Foreword

The decade of the 1970s has seen a number of major changes in the world order. The attainment of strategic equivalence between the superpowers has led their basically adversary relationship to expand increasingly into the periphery. The entry of almost fifty newly independent African countries into the world's economic and political mainstream has caused these countries increasingly to look beyond their traditional ties with Western Europe, and outside interests have begun to look toward Africa for economic and political opportunities. The result has been new actors and new areas of activity.

One of the features of the changing world order has been that several previously docile or regionally oriented countries have expanded their vision. This expansion has taken many forms, such as the quest by the developing countries for a New International Economic Order, the active role of the Group of 77, and calls for a New World Information Order. Several advanced developing countries, such as Brazil, South Korea, and Taiwan, have become competitors in markets and with technologies long assumed to be the province of the developed world. But the most significant impact has come from the newly rich oil countries, mostly of the Arab world, who have become an economic class of nations unto themselves.

This impact has come during the decade of the 1970s, most noticeably but not exclusively in the wake of the October War of 1973. The crisis of 1973 showed Arab oil producers that their oil was an important weapon and their wealth an important asset. In a matter of weeks, the Arab oil-producer cartel, the Organization of Arab Petroleum Exporting Countries (OAPEC), became a major actor on the world economic and political scene, overshadowing even its larger and better-known sister group, OPEC, which contained several non-Arab oil producers as well as the members of OAPEC. The global strategies of the superpowers and their allies had to be revised to take account of this new actor, its individual members, and their resources. For their part too, the members of OPEC, most of them Arab countries, found themselves unexpectedly on center stage. They sought to understand their new capabilities and to organize structures through which to operate. New organizations developed; old ones were revitalized.

The global involvement of the Arab oil countries was expanding; but there was also a looking inward—toward the prospects for economic and social development, and toward the need to protect their new position. This protection was especially needed in a world where, as noted above, the superpower adversary relationship was expanding into the periphery, that is, to the very structure of the Arab oil countries' global and regional relations. The result has been a strengthening of domestic defenses, a search for friends in neighboring regions, especially in Africa, and constant attention toward and concern about the activities and intentions of superpowers and their allies in Africa.

In the years before the October War, Arab countries had successfully campaigned in Africa to end the productive relationships of many countries on that continent with Israel. By 1973, however, many African nations were feeling that the Arabs had failed to compensate them sufficiently for their support. There was grumbling, and there were signs of rapprochement with Israel. But with the war, this disenchantment was quickly forgotten. Thus, while active Arab involvement and attention has been a continuing factor in contemporary African politics and economics, only recently has it begun to help extend global politics into the African continent and into the Indian Ocean region in general.

This study by Professors Le Vine and Luke analyzes the direction and dynamics of the changes in the relations between the Islamic countries and the countries of sub-Saharan Africa. It is difficult to assess the future accurately when new modes of behavior have just begun to appear. Nevertheless, this study postulates that the general model for Arab states' behavior toward Black Africa was and remains that of the Arab bankers: Saudi Arabia, Kuwait, Bahrain, and others.

Le Vine and Luke trace the evolution of Arab and African relations from their genesis in the modern period, the search for commonalities after World War II, up to and through the honeymoon of Afro-Arab solidarity. They explore African suspiciousness of Arab behavior and the important bond of Islam. The change in Arab status and the resulting redefinition of the shape of the Third World—to include an Arab developing world that belongs to the Third World but is set apart from it by wealth and new relations with the industrialized countries—are examined in light of the complex and sensitive relations that exist across and below the Sahara. Le Vine and Luke see Africa suffering as the oil-rich Arab nations exercise their power on an international scale. The development assistance provided to Africa does not make up for the import bills that mount as a result of energy needs.

Whether Africa would agree with this analysis is unclear. The events there, however, will be watched closely by the Arab countries, for whom security has become of prime importance. Since 1975, security concerns have come to the forefront of many foreign policy agendas in the Third World. The end of American involvement in Southeast Asia, the victory of the MPLA in Angola, the war in the Horn of Africa, invasions of Zaire, war again in Southeast Asia, revolution in Iran, and profound nervousness in conservative regimes throughout the Middle East point to an increased fluidity in the international system that has been interpreted differently by various analysts. Some have seen it as the experience of realized interdependence. Some view it as simply a mark of the decline in global influence for the United States and the beginning of a multilevel, multipolar international system in which multiple agendas exist for any actor, depending on the fora and the issues involved. Others believe the events of the last few years mark an international transition period in which the United States will step back from its activist involvement in the world and the USSR will move into a truly global role as the primary actor at all levels of international relations. However, the key component in these various interpretations of the contemporary period is the emphasis on security concerns in the foreign policy agendas of the Third World.

Le Vine and Luke weave a rich tapestry as they describe Arab-African relations, focusing on the economic and developmental aspects of these highly sensitive and complex contacts. Painful and pressing as the needs of development are for the African states, a major factor in the contemporary period for these emerging polities is the security roles that outside actors have traditionally played, and appear to be playing again, in regional conflicts.

Security relations among these states are a natural evolution of the full range of economic and political ties that have existed since World War II and before. However, they are also a reflection of new assessments by these Third World actors of their role in the world and the currents of the time. The militarization of African disputes by outside powers has added impetus to the arms flows to these resource-poor states at a time when development aid has lagged.

It is important for world peace that changes in the components of world order be perceived as early as possible. The Arab-African connection, as Le Vine and Luke describe it, is not a new one. However, it has begun a new phase, a phase in which it is not isolated from the entire global political environment. We cannot be sure of where that phase is headed in the 1980s, nor of where global politics will take us. Few would dispute the importance to world politics of serious activity on the part of new actors and the need for a full appreciation of the new stage. The Center for Strategic and International Studies is pleased to be able to sponsor this study as an additional building block to an understanding of the evolving world order.

Michael A. Samuels
Executive Director,
The Center for Strategic and
International Studies

Preface

This study deals with some important political and economic relationships between the independent states of Black Africa and the Arab states of the Middle East and the Mediterranean littoral. Its focus is the period between 1967 and 1978, when a new set of political and economic links was forged between the two groups of countries. The argument of the study follows the creation of the new relationship and how it developed and changed, and traces the reasons for those developments and changes. In writing the essay, we sought to avoid speculating on the virtue, or lack of virtue, of Arab and African policies; the polemical literature on such questions is quite sufficient. Our primary concern throughout was to trace a set of events whose course may have become obscured by the rhetoric of participants and analysts and to suggest how and why these events took place, and what their consequences are likely to be.

An earlier version of our study, prepared under contract as a Department of State External Research Project (contract no. 1722-72009), was completed in July 1977. During the next twelve months we gathered additional data, rethought some of our ideas, consulted widely on the details and substance of our project, and then rewrote and updated the essay. But our basic argument remains unchanged.

A number of colleagues and authorities on aspects of our subject have read drafts of parts or all of the study and offered valuable criticisms or suggestions: Harold Barnett, Hanan Aynor, Benjamin Schwadran, Naomi Chazan, and the anonymous expert who read the essay for the Center for Strategic and International Studies, Georgetown University. We gratefully acknowledge their advice and assistance. A preliminary version of our argument was presented at the 1977 meeting of the Midwest Political Science Association, and we benefited from the criticism of Ali Mazrui, a copanelist on that occasion. A particular debt of gratitude is owed to Mark Karp of Boston University for patiently explaining and clarifying some of the problems of economic analysis which we broach in Chapter 3. Victor Le Vine wishes to acknowledge the generous assistance of the Harry S. Truman Research Institute of the Hebrew University of Jerusalem, which provided research support and facilities during the Spring 1978 semester. However, none of those we consulted, nor the State Department nor the Truman Institute, are responsible for the study's analyses or conclusions: that burden remains ours, and ours alone.

VLV
TL

Abbreviations

ACPs	African, Caribbean, Pacific countries
ADF	African Development Fund
ADNOC	Abu Dhabi National Oil Company
AFDB (ADB)	African Development Bank
AFESD	Arab Fund for Economic and Social Development
AMF	Arab Monetary Fund
ARAMCO	Arabian American Oil Company
ATAFA	Arab-African Technical Assistance Fund
BADEA	Arab Bank for Economic Development in Africa
CFA	African Financial Community (Franc Zone in Africa)
CIEC	Conference on International Economic Cooperation
DAC	Development Assistance Committee
ELF	Eritrean Liberation Front
FROLINAT	Chad National Liberation Front
GSP	Generalized Scheme of Preferences
IBRD	International Bank for Reconstruction and Development (World Bank)

ICA	Integrated Commodity Agreements
IDA	International Development Agency
IDB	Islamic Development Bank
IFAD	International Fund for Agricultural Development
IMF	International Monetary Fund
INOC	Iraq National Oil Company
KFAED	Kuwait Fund for Arab Economic Development
KNOC	Kuwait National Oil Company
LDCs	Less (or Lesser, or Least) Developed Countries
MSAs	Most Seriously Affected Countries
NIEO	New International Economic Order
NIOC	National Iranian Oil Company
NODC	Non-Oil Developing Country
OAPEC	Organization of Arab Petroleum Exporting Countries
OAU	Organization of African Unity
OECD	Organization for Economic Cooperation and Development
OEEC	Organization for European Economic Co-operation
OPEC	Organization of Petroleum Exporting Countries
PLO	Palestine Liberation Organization
SAFA	Special Arab Fund for African Oil Importers
SDF	Saudi Development Fund
SDR	Special Drawing Right

TNC	transnational corporation (also known as MNC—multinational corporation)
UAE	United Arab Emirates
UNCTAD	United Nations Conference on Trade and Development
UNEO	United Nations Emergency Operation
WSLF	Western Somali Liberation Front

1
The Search for Arab-African Commonalities, 1945-73

Until well into the middle of the nineteenth century, Black Africa's relations with the Arab north African littoral and Middle East hinged on the slow spread of Islam and Arab culture into the sub-Saharan fringe and coastal East Africa, as well as on the ebb and flow of trade between the Arab world and West and East Africa. The religious and cultural mission of the Arabs tended, however, to be clouded by the Arab role in the slave trade, a role that predated European colonialism and expanded as Arab slavers became willing accomplices in the growing European share of that market. It is hardly surprising that the experience left a residue of African suspicions of Arab intentions, and, as Arye Oded (1974:34-47) and various African sources have demonstrated, that memory remains alive today in many African minds.[1] By the last third of the nineteenth century, the European colonial powers had, by and large, brought slavery to an end, and their rule had stabilized both the Islamic presence and the indigenous expressions of Arab culture. European colonialism, both in Africa and the Middle East, also placed existing Arab-African contacts on an institutionalized basis, be it within the framework of a French African empire that included the Maghreb and much of West Africa or within the larger structures of imperial European trade and political relations.

The net effect of the European presence was, on the one hand, to freeze Arab-African contacts at the official level, but, on the other, to contribute to an expansion of Islam on the continent. Pierre Rondot makes the point: "The development of means of communication, which multiplied the occasions for contact, and the expansion of trade, for which Muslims have always been particularly gifted, created conditions propitious for the spread of Islam" (1977:10). Add to this the steady growth of the numbers of African Muslims going on the *hajj* to Mecca and the extraordinary role of Al-Azhar University in training literally thousands of Black African Muslims (Cuoq, 1977:6, 7; see also Cuoq, 1975; Vermont, 1972; Ismael, 1968, 1971; Baulin, 1962; Froelich, 1965a, 1965b, 1968), and it becomes clear that by the advent of the Second World War an important Arab socioreligious presence had become commonplace in much of Black Africa.[2] That presence, of course, was not universally welcome, and in any case tended to be subject to the restraints and controls exercised by the colonial administrations.

The fifteen-year period after the end of World War II saw the emergence of nationalist movements on both sides of the Sahara and growing contact between the respective leaderships of Black African and north African groups. Initially Moroccan, Algerian, and Tunisian nationalists sought and found most of their international support among (mostly) anticolonial left French circles, as well as among the core of anticolonial sentiment organized within the United Nations. That orientation began to change as the Israelis consciously sought to leapfrog the circle of their Arab enemies by seeking friends and allies in Black Africa and, even more decisively, when Colonel Nasser, in his *Philosophy of the Revolution* (1954:69), reminded the Arab world of its obligations to and opportunities in what he called "the Second Circle—the African Continent Circle" of Arab involvement.

There is little evidence that Nasser's initial concern about Africa went beyond an interest in stimulating regional political-economic cooperation, but there is no question that he soon began to see Afro-Israeli contacts as part of a wider plan by Israel and its Western backers to stage a counterencirclement of the Arab states, something which all Arabs were duty-bound to combat (see also Cremeans, 1973:271-72; Thompson, 1969:49). Hence his continuing campaign—increasingly successful over time—to have every meeting with Africans vote resolutions on Palestine and Israel's role as a tool of Western imperialism.

It is also fair at this point to note that Nasser's reference to the African "Second Circle" was followed by an admonition that "We certainly cannot . . . relinquish our responsibility to help spread the light of knowledge and civilization to the very depth of the virgin jungles of the Continent" (Nasser, 1954:69). The sentence, which seemed to some Africans to contain unfortunate echoes of an Arab version of the European *mission civilisatrice*, served to increase rather than mitigate African suspicions. Akinsanya (1976:512-13) puts it succinctly: "The role that Nasser envisaged for Egypt in Africa smacks of a latterday version of the 'White man's burden', complete with references to Egypt's 'manifest destiny' and 'civilizing mission' in the 'interior of the Dark Continent.' " In the event, as the other north African states gained their independence one by one, contacts with African nationalists increased in number and importance.

From the African perspective, the experience of the north African nationalists provided valuable lessons in the decolonization process, and insofar as the new north African regimes projected both "radical" and anticolonial stances, a commonality of political interests could gradually emerge. That commonality, to be sure, was initially quite circumscribed; it consisted, on the one hand, of a qualified African willingness to support Arab resolutions on the Middle East conflict offered at Bandung and various subsequent African, Afro-Asian, and "nonaligned" conferences, and, on the other, of Arab support of UN and other international organizations' resolutions and decisions favoring African interests plus (after 1957) the grant of sanctuary and other assistance to a mixed lot of African "liberation" groups. This general statement does not include the more formal Arab contacts with Africa: the establishment of diplomatic relations with newly independent African states, the inclusion of Arab units within the UN force in the Congo during 1960-64 (Tunisia, Egypt, and Morocco sent troops), some trade linkages, cultural emissaries and exchanges, etc. Again, as there is already a relatively extensive literature on the character of these contacts, there is no need to detail them here

(Cremeans, 1973; Ismael, 1971; Kerekes, 1961; Mwamba, 1973); it is sufficient for our purposes to note several divergent patterns in those relations, up to 1963.

It was noted that the initial, post-1945 African-Arab contacts tended to be both circumscribed and qualified. The reasons for this lay in a combination of Arab arrogance and African suspicion, the one fostered by the unique political-cultural thrust of Arab nationalism, the other fed by old stereotypes and by what appeared to be ambiguities or contradictions in the African policies pursued by various Arab states. And throughout this period, excellent African-Israeli relations, as well as an African reluctance to become embroiled in the Middle East conflict, tended to keep African and Arab states at arm's length.

On the Arab side, Lorna Hahn (1975:4) suggests that "in some instances, the anti-colonial struggle led Arabs (particularly in North Africa) to emphasize Arab contributions to world civilization—in contrast to the apparent lack of such contributions by Black Africans—as an indication of their own fitness for independence." French use of Black African troops to control Syrian and Lebanese uprisings in 1945 and to combat Algerian revolutionaries between 1954 and 1962 helped to create some anti-African feeling, as did the visible reluctance of African nationalists to join the anti-Israeli camp in exchange for Arab support of their causes. Nasser best expressed the underlying Arab view: the Arabs (in particular, the Egyptians) were Africa's natural leaders, a point suggesting no small measure of cultural and political chauvinism. "The U.A.R.," said Nasser, "has the responsibility of leading the fight for liberty and economic progress in Africa" (quoted in Baulin, 1962:44). African leaders, for their part, often found it difficult to overlook what seemed to be Arab airs of superiority, and in any case disputed Arab claims to leadership in the African nationalist struggle. That claim was finally laid to rest at the First African Summit Conference in Addis Ababa in 1963 (at which the Organization of African Unity was founded), but not before the epitome of the dispute—the rivalry between Nasser and Nkrumah—had helped to foster important divisions within the African camp (Thompson, 1969; Legum 1965). Again, the details need not detain us here; what is important to note is that the most significant of these divisions, that between the so-called moderate (the Monrovia bloc) and radical African states (the Casablanca bloc) contained an Arab dimension that served to exacerbate rather than mitigate the split. Briefly recalled, the latter bloc was the outcome of a conference in Casablanca at the beginning of 1961 of the heads of state of Morocco, Egypt, Ghana, Guinea, and Mali, the provisional government of Algeria, and the representatives of Libya and Ceylon. Libya seems to have attended by mistake, and Ceylon was clearly odd man out, but the group drew up a charter characterized by a series of aggressively political—even "radical"—postures on such questions as the UN's involvement in the Congo, the liquidation of imperialism and neocolonialism, and nonalignment. The conference also favored intensified efforts to create a joint African High Command of Chiefs of Staff, an idea which made the Egyptians unhappy "because Ghana's armed forces were still officered by Britons and trained by Israelis, with whom Egypt could hardly be expected to cooperate and share military information" (Jansen, 1966:275). It was one of the few discordant notes struck at the conference. Apart from statements of common purpose, to please Morocco, the group denounced Mauritania, a member of the Monrovia group and against which Morocco then had territorial claims; "and to please the three Arab states, the group denounced Israel, with whom many of the Monrovia states (and Ghana)" had "good relations" (Jansen, 1966:275).

Perhaps most significant for the "moderate" African states, the Casablanca alliance not only crystallized a much more radical view of pan-Africanism than the one they shared, but also provided legitimacy for a campaign of violent political subversion against them espoused by Ghana, Guinea, and Mali, and now joined by three north African Arab states. By 1957, Egypt had already become a major center for African political exiles—providing them with quarters, logistical and financial help, military training, and access to Radio Free Africa, which beamed their messages to all parts of the continent (Ismael, 1971; Tibi, 1971). It can hardly have been reassuring to the "moderates" that among the groups receiving

aid from Nasser were exiles from such Monrovia states as
Cameroon, Gabon, Congo/Brazzaville, the Ivory Coast,
Senegal, Niger, Nigeria, and Mauritania. After 1961, Algeria
and Morocco also offered both haven and assistance to many of
these same exiles.

Thus, it was not surprising that when, in 1963, President
Nkrumah—with quiet Arab help—sought to push his views on
continental political unity at Addis Ababa, he was rebuffed by
the majority of African states. The Arabs were barely able to
mention their favorite topic (Egyptian Foreign Minister Fawzy
declared that he had not raised, nor would he raise, the issue of
Israel), and even Nasser now took the opportunity to reverse
course, asserting that economic integration must come before
political unity and offering himself as a disinterested mediator
in African disputes (Woronoff, 1970:125-54; Jansen, 1966:351-
66).

It is fair to say that Addis probably represented the nadir of
postwar African-Arab relations. Even Nkrumah, who had
broken with Nasser soon after Casablanca (without also
offering reconciliation to his neighbors), now declared the end
of the Casablanca bloc and joined his Guinean and Malien
colleagues in the new Organization of African Unity. The
Moroccans and Algerians offered similar olive branches. The
net effect of all these moves, and of the patent victory of the
Monrovia bloc, was to isolate Egypt, increase African
suspicions of Arab intentions, and, to visible Arab dismay,
vindicate African-Israeli ties. Yet, in four years the situation
was to change drastically again, resulting in the inauguration
of a new period of close Arab-African relations. We turn briefly
to the dynamics of that change.

Patently, the new era began in 1967, with the June Arab-
Israeli war marking the turning point. To be sure, just before,
during, and immediately after the June war, most African states
remained openly sympathetic to Israel, even rejecting initiatives for a special meeting of the OAU on the Middle Eastern
situation. By the time the special UN session met in mid-June
at the request of the Soviet Union, the African positions had
begun to shift as new cross-pressures were brought to bear, but
not sufficiently to prevent some seventeen of the thirty-two sub-

Saharan states from voting for a nominally "pro-Israeli" Latin American resolution. The defections, however, were notable: Zambia, Congo/Kinshasa, and Tanzania, hitherto considered securely pro-Israeli and grateful recipients of Israeli aid, all voted "No" on the Latin American resolution. Tanzania's Nyerere, long a friend of Israel, not only offered aid to Nasser "in defense of your rights against imperialism," but in the UN thereafter followed a consistently pro-Arab line. (Tanzania did not, however, break diplomatic relations or expel Israeli technicians until later.) Guinea did break relations with Israel in 1967, and the governments of Mali, Mauritania, and Somalia issued strongly pro-Arab statements before and after the war. Also at the June UN meetings, Burundi, Congo/Brazzaville, Senegal, Uganda, and Zambia (as well as Guinea, Mali, Mauritania, and Tanzania) voted in favor of a "nonaligned" Yugoslav (read Russian) resolution generally considered pro-Arab; Nigeria and Gabon also supported the resolution, but equivocally (Decalo, 1967:57-61). (A virulently anti-Israel resolution introduced by Albania, which, among other things, implicated the U.S. and Britain in "premeditated armed aggression," received only one African vote—that of Mauritania.)

As time passed, direct and indirect African support for Israel in the UN, the OAU, and at various international conferences began to wane. By September 1973, when the Fourth Non-Aligned Summit Conference met in Algiers, representatives from thirty-four African and eighteen Arab states agreed on a strong resolution condemning both Zionism and Israel. From Algiers, many heads of state proceeded to New York for the opening of the UN General Assembly, where attacks on Zionism and Israel increased, and more African states began to announce breaks with Israel.[3] On October 6, the "Yom Kippur–10 Ramadan" War was started, and the list of African states breaking relations with Israel grew even longer. By mid-November 1973, all African states with the exceptions of Malawi, Lesotho, Swaziland, and Mauritius had severed their ties with Israel. To the partisans of these developments, the marriage between Africans and Arabs had finally been consummated, and the future could only bring blessings for all concerned. Even Ali Mazrui, who from time to time felt the need to remind the Arabs that their best friends are Africans, saw in these (and later) events a process whereby the Middle East and Africa had begun to merge "into a single international subsystem" (1975b:30).

2
1973-78: The Honeymoon and
Its Unhappy Aftermath

Clearly, by the end of 1973 Arabs and Africans appeared to have found the commonality that had so long eluded them. Arab and—at least initially—African analysts of the Afro-Arab rapprochement have tended to see it as the result of a combination of factors, all of which point to what amounted to successful conversion of each side to the other's most urgent causes and preoccupations. The Africans, it has been argued, had now come to appreciate the Arab position in the conflict with Israel, to understand the true nature of Israel as an agent of imperialism, and to see the justice of the Palestinian cause. The Arabs, for their part, now saw the significance of the struggle in southern Africa, the need for African unity and solidarity, and the real dimensions of the Western neocolonialist threat to the continent. Both sides could now share in the benefits conferred by unity in a common struggle against common enemies.[4]

We maintain that these explanations contain some small reflections of reality—but not much more. By and large, they appear to be post hoc rationalizations, concealing a much more complex interplay of self-interested policies and behaviors. We argue that though the *catalyst* for the change was a dramatic, qualitative change in the Arab-Israeli conflict, it was the extraordinary success of Arab diplomacy in Africa, coupled with Israeli difficulties and the Arabs' shrewd use of money and oil as weapons of political and economic persuasion, that ultimately led to the new alliance.

The Israelis undoubtedly contributed, albeit unwillingly, to the Arab-African rapprochement. The Israeli presence in

Africa, motivated in part by an effort to seek allies in its quest
for a negotiated settlement of its dispute with the Arabs,
eventually became counterproductive. For one thing, as Israeli
officials involved in the effort now admit, Israel undoubtedly
overextended itself by attempting too many projects in too
many places, was unable to provide complementary capital
backing for some projects it helped plan and actually initiated,
and, in general, found it difficult to say no when asked to join
in projects of doubtful merit or with political overtones. Thus,
Israel probably helped raise expectations about its assistance
that it could only partially, or not at all, fulfill. Also, as Richard
Bissell observes, however useful the Israelis made themselves in
Africa, their extended presence made them available as
scapegoats for developmental failures, the multiplication of
military coups d'etat, and increasingly unfavorable balances of
trade. "To some degree, Israel suffered simply because her
diplomats had been in Africa long enough to make enemies"
(1976:159; see also Kreinin, 1964; Amir, 1974; Gitelson, 1976).
Bissell's argument may seem somewhat simplistic, but it still
makes considerable sense. Where, for example, Israel had
helped train paramilitary or military elements in various
African countries and these were involved in coups, Israel
could be blamed. Where Israeli advisers had helped set up
cooperatives and these failed, Israel could be blamed. Where
Israeli advisers had helped build and run tourist hotels and not
enough tourists showed up to make them economically viable,
Israel could be blamed. The reason is simple: the Israeli
connection was always inherently vulnerable because it was
always politically marginal at best. It could, and did, become a
liability when more serious interests were engaged. Israeli
political miscues also helped. Certainly, the fact of close
cooperation between Israel and South Africa, where a sizable
Jewish minority had even provided Israel with support in its
military struggles, could easily be exploited to demonstrate
putative similarities and links between apartheid and Zionism.
Israel also made the mistake of backing unpopular losers: for
example, it provided aid to Biafra, and it maintained good
relations with prerevolutionary Portugal, because of the
usefulness of the Azores as a supply base (see in particular

Mazrui, 1975b). To be sure, all of these connections might have appeared justified to the Israelis, but they could hardly have been expected to please their African friends, and once seized upon and magnified by Arab propagandists, what once could have been considered forgivable errors of policy began to register as part of a pattern of outrageous and gross anti-African conduct (von Schack, 1977:112). Consequently, an Israeli connection became a convenient sacrifice to offer radical groups and intellectuals who had become enamored of the Palestinian cause, and the expulsion of Israeli diplomats and technicians a low-cost way of making a symbolic break with the West without disrupting the principal financial flows into Africa (Gitelson, 1974:451-84). Finally, the magnitude of the Israeli victory in 1967 and the Israelis' propensity to crow over it not only offended some African sensibilities but shifted the Israeli image from underdog (for whom sympathy came naturally) to dangerous "overdog." And Arab propagandists wasted no time in labeling the Arab defeat as a victory for the imperialist West, a point not lost on Israel's African friends.

Even more significant than the Israeli predicament were the Arabs' diplomatic initiatives in Africa itself. It is often forgotten that King Feisal of Saudi Arabia made *two* trips to Africa, the first in 1966 and the second, more publicized visit in November 1972. The September 1966 visit took Feisal to Morocco, Guinea, Mali, and Tunisia, ostensibly on behalf of an Islamic conference he advocated. It should be noted that the communiqués following the king's visits to Guinea and Mali contained not only affirmations of Islamic unity, but also pledges that the three countries would continue to support the Arab people of Palestine in the fight for the liberation of their country (*West Africa*, no. 2473:1105). It is not known if Feisal made any promises to the leaders of Mali or Guinea, but his visit clearly became part of a larger pattern of increased contacts between Arab states and predominantly Muslim African countries. Feisal's trip was followed by official visits to Saudi Arabia and Kuwait by Niger's President Hamani Diori (November 1966), to Saudi Arabia by Sudan's President Al-Azhari (December 1966), to Algeria by Senegal's President Senghor (February 1967), and by the "Little Summit" of

"Revolutionary African States" in Cairo (April 1967), attended by the heads of state of Egypt, Algeria, Tanzania, and Mauritania and by delegations from Guinea, Mali, and the Congo People's Republic. Feisal's October 14-29, 1972, tour took him to Uganda, Chad, Senegal, Mauritania, and Niger; this time the communiqués unequivocally called for support of both African and Palestinian liberation movements and denounced Zionist evils, designs, and expansionism not only in Palestine but in the world at large. By this time, moreover, the Ninth Assembly of OAU Heads of State (meeting in Rabat in June) had already passed the strongest anti-Israeli resolutions ever approved by that body, and Uganda had just severed relations with Israel (in April). In any case, the conclusion is inescapable that the Feisal mission was explicitly undertaken to further the Arab goal of wooing the Africans to the Arab side and that any promises he made would be seconded by other Arab states, particularly by Libya.

Within days of Feisal's departure from Fort-Lamy on November 27, Chad's President Tombalbaye broke relations with Israel, and Israel announced that it was closing its embassies in Niger (November 29) and the Congo People's Republic. To be sure, there is no visible evidence that Feisal offered his African hosts any inducements to break their ties with Israel, but it can hardly have been a coincidence that following a three-day visit to Libya by Chad's President Tombalbaye (in December), a $91.2 million Libyan loan to Chad was announced (*West Africa*, no. 2900:55).

Marie Sirkin (1975) provides evidence that by late 1972, Chad was on the verge of bankruptcy and that it had failed to get funds from either France or Israel to prevent financial disaster. President Tombalbaye then broke relations with Israel and flew to Tripoli and the friendly arms of President Qaddhafi. Tombalbaye's visit to Libya was not without its ironies. On September 6, 1971, Tombalbaye had broken diplomatic relations with Libya and attacked the Libyan government for allegedly instigating an attempted coup against his regime on August 27 of that year. The Libyans, in their turn, had denounced Tombalbaye as the tool of the Israeli ambassador in Fort-Lamy, formally recognized the FROLINAT rebels, and warned of Zionist conspiracies in Chad and elsewhere in Africa. (Libya also apparently promised to curtail its support of Chadian FROLINAT rebels, and Chad invited the PLO to open an office in its capital.) Earlier in 1972, in March, Uganda also had broken with Israel, and in rather spectacular fashion. That event followed a February visit to Libya by Uganda's Idi Amin, during which he evidently obtained assurances of substantial benefits if he broke with Israel. Those subsequently included not only circa $18 million in development aid from Libya and Saudi Arabia and a $15 million loan from the Saudis (ARB/EFT, 1972:2433), but also (it is believed) a promise of some $16 million to Idi Amin himself "to be channeled through the Kampala branch of the Libyan Commercial Bank, as well as better publicized military assistance" (*Africa Confidential*, 1972:5). It should also be noted that, like Tombalbaye, Idi Amin was heavily in debt, perhaps by as much as $220 million. Severance of the Israeli tie meant, for both presidents, cancellation of the Israeli part of their debts; in Uganda's case this involved around 10 percent of the total. Another part of Libyan quid pro quo became evident in September 1972 when some 420 Libyan soldiers were sent to Uganda when anti-Amin elements invaded the country from Tanzania.

The use of Arab—and especially Libyan—finances to help the Arab diplomatic offensive seems to have had its desired effect by mid-1973. Again, the connection between anti-Israeli policies and Arab largess was never spelled out in so many words, but given the evidence it would be naive to think that the substantial Arab aid given Chad, Uganda, Niger, Mali, Congo/Brazzaville, Senegal, and Burundi was provided solely on the basis of disinterested philanthropy.

Other events in the interim obviously played a role in creating the new Arab-African links. There was, for example, the visit to Egypt and Israel of the four African "wise men" (Presidents Ahidjo of Cameroon, Senghor of Senegal, Mobutu Sese Seko of Zaire, and General Gowon of Nigeria) sent under OAU auspices in November 1971 to try to revive the Jarring Mission. The four came under strong Arab pressure at the 1972 OAU Summit, even though their report had been moderate in tone, and most of them reverted to a position condemning Israel. Then too, Israel continued to maintain both trade and friendly relations with South Africa, in the face of a mounting campaign against that country by the African states. Finally, it is difficult to overlook the cumulative effect of Arab pressures—both bilateral and within international forum—and the impact of what, by mid-1973, had begun to look like a wild rush to the Arab side. Those who hitherto had not shifted found it hard to continue to resist the increasingly hard-line resolutions passed at the OAU, in the UN, and in other bodies, as well as the persuasive example of African states who had visibly profited by espousing the Arab cause. After October 1973, however, the rush—at least in Israeli eyes— became a stampede.

Rivlin and Fomerand suggest that Israel's occupation during the October war of a portion of Egyptian territory on the west bank of the Suez Canal also provided the Arabs with a new talking point: "The Arab-Israeli conflict was no longer purely regional; it had become an issue affecting the entire African continent because of Israel's 'threat to African soil.' Statements justifying diplomatic breaks with Israel are replete with this argument" (1976:347). Add to this the Arab exploitation of the fact that the United states had used Portuguese possessions to resupply Israel, the constant identification of Israel with South Africa, plus the Arab claim that they had won a stunning victory, and the Africans' massive shift to the Arab side becomes readily understandable. Ali Mazrui disparages the contention that the African states broke with Israel "for the sake of cheaper oil from the Arabs." By the time OPEC dramatically raised the price of oil, he points out, most African states had already sided with the Arabs. Rather, he feels their conversion can be ascribed to ideological radicalism, or to belief in the Arab cause for its merits, or partly to religious identification, or (as in the cases of "moderate" states like Kenya, the Ivory Coast, and Ethiopia) partly to their feeling that they "did not want to be isolated from the continental African diplomatic trends or break ranks with other members of the OAU" (1975a:736). Nigeria is the case that best supports the thesis of a break with Israel for the sake of African solidarity. Nigeria did not sever the Israeli tie when the October war broke out, waiting until October 25 to do so. Moreover, that action came as somewhat of a surprise, since General Gowon had, on October 9, debunked the idea of doing precisely that. By October 22, however, Nigeria (Gowon was the OAU's current chairman) could hold out no longer, since most of the other moderate African states had already cut their links with Israel and Israel appeared to be in violation of Security Council Resolution 343 (of October 22). Finally there were unconfirmed reports that South Africa had sent arms to Israel to help it against the Arabs. It should be noted that however well Nigeria (and probably Gabon as well) fits the "African solidarity" thesis, Nigeria is probably something of a deviant case since it was one of the two African states not susceptible to oil blackmail. Moreover, there must have been pressure from within the ranks of OPEC as well. Certainly Nigeria, as a member of the oil cartel, gained much more than it lost by going along with its OPEC brethren.

Both sets of arguments admittedly identify factors that certainly helped African states justify their massive rally to the Arab cause; yet it is fair to point out that (1) the early converts indisputably displayed more economic and political oppor- tunism than ideological affinity, and (2) the circumstances under which most of the rest switched suggest they did so as a consequence of extreme pressure—it was not moral, religious, or political conversion. While it is true that the "dramatic" fourfold rise in the price of oil occurred after most African states had broken with Israel, it is also true that on October 8 (before eighteen African states announced breaks with Israel) the OPEC producers proposed a 70 percent rise in the price of oil, that on October 16 they unilaterally raised the price by 70 percent (Libya raised it by 94 percent), and that the oil embargo itself was announced on October 17, a date prior to the break by sixteen African states. Moreover, at the OPEC Vienna meetings September 15-16, they already had agreed to seek at least a 50 percent lump increase in posted prices. In any event, the Arab oil producers had made no secret of their desire and intent to raise the price of oil; beginning in 1970 with President Qaddhafi's raises, the pattern had been there for all to see.

We think it disingenuous at best to argue that oil diplomacy had little or no role to play in the African switch.[5] Rather, we agree with Marie Sirkin that "the biggest immediate factor was without question the fear on the part of most Africans that they would face a complete cutoff of their petroleum if they did not take immediate action to isolate Israel and express their solidarity with the Arab cause. There was no subtlety in the Arab threat. It was clearly and openly expressed not only to the Africans but to everyone else" (1975:23). Given the fact that the industrial nations of the West unequivocally expressed their vulnerability to the Arabs, it "is little wonder that the African states seemed to rush in a panic to gain Arab grace" (Sirkin, 1975:23). Senegal's President Senghor, unwittingly speaking for most Third World and Western countries, put the proposition bluntly and clearly: "The Arabs have numbers, space, and oil. . . ; they outweigh Israel" (cited by Rivlin and Fomerand, 1976:347).

It is also possible, after 1967, that radical Arab terrorism may have helped create a general sense of insecurity among African leaders and thus added to the political and economic pressures upon them. There is no direct evidence to support this point, but the uncomfortable—and unexpected—proximity of various acts of Arab terrorism (e.g., ELF hijackings in Ethiopia and North Africa, the skyjacking of an Air Afrique plane, the murder of three diplomats—one Belgian, two Americans—in Khartoum by Black September guerillas, the open assistance by Palestinians to Idi Amin's army, etc.), plus the presence of agents of Arab-Palestinian groups in various African capitals (Fatah, for example, had offices in Dar es Salaam, Kampala, and Lusaka by the beginning of 1973), as well as the fact that several African liberation groups had direct ties with Palestinian organizations or had been infiltrated by them, all probably helped convince African leaders that prudence dictated renunciation of the Israeli link and wholesale espousal of the Arab cause. Finally, persistent rumors—which begin to sound credible because they have been repeatedly and privately confirmed by reputable, highly placed Africans at the UN and elsewhere—suggest that there may also have been actual intimidation, including veiled and not-so-veiled threats by some of the more radical Arab leaders and their agents against African leaders themselves. The Libyans are most frequently mentioned in this connection.

Were the Africans promised anything in exchange for their conversion? The Arabs say no, but African commentators, in expressing disappointment about the quantity and quality of Arab largess, recently have said or implied that they at least expected guaranteed supplies of oil, reasonable or concessionary prices, sizable Arab capital investment, and assistance that would somehow offset the expected drain on their exchange reserves occasioned by the higher prices they would have to pay for oil. For example, Mazrui notes: "Some black Africans expected special rewards from the Arabs following their break with Israel. The rise of oil prices of course placed African economies under severe strain, and when OPEC refused to consider a two-tier price system for Africa, frustrations ensued. In Nairobi in June 1974 it was even suggested in the East African Legislative Assembly that the Nile River be diverted by the East African states so that they could then sell its water to the Arabs, in exchange for barrels of oil" (1975a:738). Akinsanya observes: "Thus, when . . . [OAPEC] decided to use Arab oil as a weapon to alter some major powers' policies toward Israel, African states hoped they would be spared the adverse effects of the oil embargo. . . . African countries wanted their oil supplies to be guaranteed, and hoped they would not have to pay high prices for oil which would exhaust their meagre foreign exchange earnings" (1976:525-26). Bamisaye, in discussing the financial implications of oil-dollar accumulation in a few, primarily Arab, hands, suggests that, "For the present, the Africans have not got much to show for the political support given to the Arabs over the Arab-Israeli confrontation" (1974:15; see also Chibwe, 1976:42-50). In sum, given the weight of circumstantial evidence and testimony, it seems highly probable that by word—or at least by deed—the Arabs intimated that their African friends would not be disadvantaged by their switch. In all likelihood, the Arabs must have recognized that promises of support for African causes would not be enough to offset the inevitable, eventual resentment against the harsh pressures of oil diplomacy; they would have to "sweeten the pot." In any case, there is no doubt that the Africans *expected* some sort of financial and economic quid pro quo; their later unhappiness was obviously rooted mainly in that perception.

The new alliance certainly bore some fruit for both sides. For the Arabs, it meant automatic majorities in the assemblies of the UN and its ancillary bodies on any issue touching the Middle East. It prompted Idi Amin, on October 1, 1975, to appeal to the United States "to rid their society of the Zionists"; it permitted the dramatic UN appearance of Yasir Arafat in November 1974 to plead the PLO case and gave that organization observer status, entitled to participate as an equal in all Middle East–related discussions; it assured that anti-Zionist, pro-Palestinian resolutions would be passed at the 1974 and 1975 UNESCO meetings, at the 1975 International Women's Year Conference in Mexico City, and at the Habitat Conference in Canada, not to mention the annual meetings of the OAU and other international bodies. It gave impetus to a move—eventually unsuccessful—to expel Israel from the UN, and it worked to assure the withdrawal of South Africa from that organization. And on November 11, 1975, it operated—though somewhat imperfectly—to mobilize nineteen African votes of the seventy that approved the UN General Assembly's resolution that identified Zionism as "a form of racism." The full list is much longer; it is sufficient for our purposes to make the point that the new alliance served to emphasize the Arabs' contention that their new power did not rest just on oil, and that their aims were seconded by most of the Third World states. For the Africans, it meant material aid to the OAU's Liberation Committee, immediate extension of the oil embargo to Rhodesia and South Africa along with support for resolutions condemning these two countries, and the prospect of help to pay oil bills as well as new sources of capital and development aid.

Impressive as these reciprocities were, it already had become clear by the spring of 1974 that the new alliance contained marked asymmetries: although the Arabs spoke of granting development aid to offset higher oil prices, the oil producers had no intention of selling oil to African consumers at concessionary prices. Arab aid was slow in coming while, at the same time, the OPEC-imposed prices rose steadily. African foreign-exchange reserves dwindled, trade deficits grew, and African discontent over this situation mounted.

The oil producers first responded by creating the Arab Bank for Economic Development in Africa (BADEA) in November 1973 with an initial capital of $231 million (raised to $500 million in August 1975). This was to provide concessional development loans only to non-Arab African countries. The BADEA was followed in December 1973 by the $15 million Arab-African Technical Assistance Fund (ATAFA) and in January 1974 by the $265 million Special Arab Fund for African Oil Importers (SAFA), designed to provide long-term credits carrying 1 percent interest. In June 1974 the Islamic Development Bank (IDB) was set up with a capital of $2.4 billion; though intended principally to help Arab states, it was also expected to aid African countries with Muslim majorities. In addition, the oil producers set up their own $800 million OPEC Special Fund (January 1976) to make soft loans to countries with balance-of-payments difficulties, made contributions to the African Development Bank (AFDB) and the African Development Fund (ADF), and bolstered the aid-giving capabilities of the older Kuwait Fund for Arab Economic Development (KFAED) and Saudi Development Fund (SDF). In addition, the principal Arab oil producers negotiated bilateral concessional (with up to a 25 percent grant element) and nonconcessional aid to African countries. Finally, six Arab nations and Oman underwrote some 87 percent of the capitalization of the International Monetary Fund's (IMF) special Oil Facility in 1974-75, and 60 percent of its funds for 1975-76. The Oil Facility provided Special Drawing Rights (1 SDR = U.S. $1.15) to finance balance-of-payments deficits for those nations most seriously affected by the increased price of OPEC oil. In 1974 and 1975 the Arab oil producers and Iran committed $347.5 million in bilateral concessional aid to African countries, $350.3 million in bilateral nonconcessional aid, and $706.5 million to African and Islamic funds (BADEA, ATAFA, IDB), plus their contributions to the IMF special Oil Facility and the World

Bank—a $2.1 billion "aid transfer." (See, particularly, *African Development*, 1975:24-27; Asfahany, 1977. For details on these agencies, see Chapter 4.)

In all, the Arab response—summarized above—seemed not only generous, but designed to correct the asymmetries about which the African states had complained at the beginning of 1974. Yet by the end of 1976, the Arab-African alliance had become so tenuous that African states had begun not only to drop hints that some of them were reconsidering their stand on Israel, but also to complain aloud about uncompensated oil-price increases, OPEC harshness, and Arab stinginess (Mazrui, 1975a; Akinsanya, 1976; Bamisaye, 1974; *Africa Currents*, 1976:1-8). A pledge of $1.45 billion in aid to Africa (the Africans had demanded $2.2 billion) by Saudi Arabia and three other Arab oil producers at the Afro-Arab Summit Conference in Cairo on March 7, 1977, probably salvaged the alliance through 1977, but the signs of its disintegration were clearly present. (The Cairo Summit is discussed at greater length in this study, pp. 64 to 67.) What happened, it is now clear, is that the African states had come to realize that instead of being beneficiaries of their alliance with the Arabs, they had, in fact, become net losers. Only several elements of this development need be cited to help make the point:

• The African states have received neither concessions nor other special considerations on the price of the oil they buy. As a consequence, all but those who are themselves oil producers (Nigeria, Gabon, and Angola), or who have been able to offset the drain on their treasuries by getting higher prices for their exports, have had to spend up to 35 percent of their budgets for imported oil. During 1974, 1975, and 1976, most of the African countries in the UN's "most seriously affected" (MSA) category suffered serious balance-of-payments problems largely attributable to oil-price increases, and some went heavily into debt as a result (OECD, 1975 and 1976; *National Journal*, 1976:1722-79; IMF/IFS, 1975 and 1976). Tanzania, for example, had to seek $250 million in 1975 to help overcome its deficits.

Further, the effects of the oil-price increases have tended to be cumulative, representing a drain on both the actual and the potential resources of the African (and non-African) MSAs.

K. A. Hammeed has argued that the cumulative drain is the sum of (1) the drain of resources due to the extra costs of oil imports, plus (2) the drain of resources due to increased costs of other imports, plus (3) the loss of export earnings due to lower growth in developed countries, plus (4) the loss of share(s) in direct international investment due to competition from oil-exporting countries for such investment (1976:353; see also *Afro-Asian News*, 1975). In the case of almost all African MSAs, these effects were represented by a precipitate decline in official foreign reserves and assets, heavy borrowing from domestic and foreign sources, and increasing inability to capitalize any but the most modest development projects. Most important, the crisis not only placed additional financial burdens on most African economies but, in a number of instances, undermined economies already heavily impacted by other, unrelated factors such as drought, political instability, earlier debt, governmental mismanagement, and the like. (Chapter 3 examines the question of effects in greater detail.)

● Most of the Arab-OPEC aid has gone to non-oil-producing Arab states, or to African states with predominantly Muslim populations. During 1974, eight such African states (of nineteen) received 90 percent of Middle East concessional bilateral aid; in 1975, they accounted for 86.9 percent. Of the twelve African states that received nonconcessional bilateral aid, five—all Muslim countries—accounted for 85 percent of the totals committed in 1974 and 1975 (MEED, 4/13/77:39). Arab countries subscribed 41 percent of the African Development Bank's capital to December 31, 1975; however, they only accounted for 37.3 percent of the total (some $65.9 of $176.6 million) actually paid in, and they borrowed $71.4 million, that is, $5.5 million more than they gave. Arab contributions constituted 16.7 percent of the African Development Fund's subscriptions to the end of 1975; in 1974, 65.8 percent, in 1975, 40 percent, and in 1976, 45.8 percent of the Fund's loans went to Muslim countries (U.S. Senate *Hearings*, 1976:35 and 1977:31). Similar patterns have prevailed for loans provided by all the Arab funds except SAFA. A United Nations Conference on Trade and Development report on OPEC aid confirms the trend:

Nevertheless, the concentration on Arab recipients in bilateral concessional flows is still considerable. In absolute terms, total flows of concessional disbursements to non-Arab countries were less than $800 million in 1974 and less than $300 million during the first half of 1975. This helps to explain why only slightly less than two-thirds of these flows go to the most seriously affected countries, of which Egypt alone accounted for about one half in 1974 and for as much as 64 percent during the first half of 1975. . . . In fact, only 23 of the 42 most seriously affected countries received any bilateral concessional disbursements from OPEC donors during the period under review (UNCTAD, 1977:5).

The period covered by the report, issued in 1977, is 1973 through June 1975. The actual figures, for both concessional and nonconcessional aid during this period, made the point with dramatic clarity. (Table 1 summarizes these data and some nominal analysis.) In the 1973-75 period, when the need for compensatory aid to the weak African economies was greatest, the African members of the Arab League received nearly 90 percent of all OPEC aid going to less developed African countries (LDCs), and, of that, nearly 74 percent went to Egypt. Virtually all the Arab-OPEC countries' aid to Africa was channeled through bilateral conduits or disbursed through the Arab League. By way of contrast, the IMF Oil Facility, 87 percent financed by OPEC in 1974-75 and 60 percent in 1975-76 and 1977-78, achieved a much less skewed distribution: the non–Arab League African states received 72.2 percent of the African total for the 1973-75 period. (As a matter of fact, Arab League and other Muslim countries only received 15.6 percent of the total drawings on the Facility to January 31, 1978.) Overall, most sources agree that non-Muslim states of the poor Third World have received less than 10 percent of the total OPEC concessional aid since 1973. The point is simple: considerations of religion and regional politics strongly override the criterion of need in determining aid recipients.

• Much of the OPEC-Arab aid disbursed to multilateral institutions to help alleviate oil-induced balance-of-payments strains (mainly to the IMF Oil Facility) has gone to hard-hit industrialized nations, such as Italy and Great Britain, instead of to African countries with proportionally equal, or worse, problems. (Through January 31, 1978, Western European countries accounted for 62.4 percent of the drawings on the Facility.) Moreover, most of that aid has been nonconcessional; the loans to the IMF Oil Facility, for example, carry an average interest rate of about 7.5 percent. In another case, the $2.1 billion OPEC "aid transfer" to the World Bank in 1974 actually involved the purchase of the IBRD's interest-bearing bonds.

Also, the *terms* of the Arab-OPEC aid generally hardened from 1974 to 1975, and in fact, according to the Organization for Economic Cooperation and Development's Maurice Williams, "the hardest terms, both in 1974 and 1975, were often extended to the poorest countries, those with a GNP per capita below $200, while the softest terms in 1975 benefited the richest recipients, i.e., with GNP per capita over $1000" (OECD, 1976:100-101). (The former group includes twenty-six African states, that is, most of the United Nations Emergency Operation's twenty-one African "most seriously affected" countries, plus Malawi, the Gambia, Togo, Botswana, and Swaziland.) Not only are interest rates high on aid loans to the MSAs but the grant element in the OPEC countries' concessional aid commitments has dropped from 74 percent in 1973 to 38 percent in 1975, compared to an increase from 66 percent to 69 percent by the DAC countries (OECD, 1976:101).

The net result of this Arab bounty has been to increase, not mitigate, the African LDCs' debt burden, and all to the principal profit of the Arab oil producers. African states thus affected cannot fail to note that they pay their Arab friends twice for oil: an excessively high price on delivery, then interest on the money they borrow to pay for it. Thus, the Africans argue "that while the West has been assisted by Arab loans, with concessionary interest rates of about 5 percent [they] have to borrow the same funds on the Eurodollar market, often at 15-20 percent interest" (MEED, 4/3/77:7).

"Fifteen-twenty percent interest" is an obvious exaggeration, but the point behind it is not: since the OPEC nations are now the main net suppliers of funds to the Euromarket, African borrowers of Eurodollars are more than likely to have to apply to the generous, high-interest left hand of the same Arab

TABLE 1

GROSS RECEIPTS OF AFRICAN DEVELOPING COUNTRIES FROM OPEC SOURCES[a]

(in millions of US$)

Recipients	1973	1974	Jan.-Je. 1975	1973-75	(Drawings on) IMF OIL FACILITY TO 1-31-78[b]
I. African members of the Arab League[c]	680.73	1,307.33	1,253.99	3,242.05	152.0
(Of which Egypt)	(580.09)	(934.76)	(1,154.83)	(2,669.68)	
II. All other African recipients[a]	30.73	277.47	67.77	375.97	394.2
Totals, all Africa	711.46	1,584.80	1,321.76	3,618.02	546.2
III. Total receipts for all developing countries (LDC's)	1,1176.9	3,437.38	2,344.53	7,958.70	2,538.9
IV. Analyses of Nos. I-III					
No. I as % of all LDC's	60.9	38.0	53.4	40.7	
No. II as % of all LDC's	2.7	8.1	2.9	4.7	
No. I as % of all African countries	95.7	82.5	94.9	89.6	

No. II as % of all African countries	4.3	17.5	5.1	10.4
Egypt as % of all LDC's	51.9	27.1	49.25	33.5
Egypt as % of all African countries	81.5	60.0	87.3	73.8

SOURCES: United Nations Conference for Trade and Development (UNCTAD) (1976). Handbook of International Trade and Development Statistics. New York: UN/UNCTAD. 322-23. International Monetary Fund (IMF). International Financial Statistics XXXI, 2 (March 1978):10-11.

NOTES: a. Includes concessional and non-concessional loans, contributions, etc., provided bilaterally or through such multilateral agencies as the Arab Fund for Loans to African Countries, the Arab Fund for Social and Economic Development, the OAPEC special account for Arab petro-importing countries, the U.N. Special Account.

b. The IMF oil facility includes the original (1974), a second (1975), and third (the so-called "Witteveen") replenishment. OPEC provided 87% of the 1974 and 60% of the 1975.

c. Algeria, Egypt, Mauritania, Morocco, Somalia, Sudan, Tunisia, and Libya. (Libya, while a member of OPEC, is included because it received $0.04 million in 1974.)

d. Benin, Botswana, Burundi, Cameroon, Chad, Central African Republic, Equatorial Guinea, Ethiopia, Gambia, Ghana, Guinea, Guinea-Bissau, Ivory Coast, Kenya, Lesotho, Liberia, Madagascar, Malawi, Mali, Niger, Rwanda, Senegal, Sierra Leone, Swaziland, Tanzania, Togo, Uganda, Upper Volta, Zaire, Zambia. Countries not listed were members of OPEC (Nigeria, Gabon), or had received no OPEC aid during the period, or were not yet independent at the time.

banker-states whose low-interest right hand showed earlier parsimony in providing "aid." (According to the *Banker* of March 1977, the OPEC states were net suppliers to the Euromarket of some $33 billion by September 1976[1977:119].)

• Bilateral Arab aid actually disbursed seldom exceeds between 35 percent to 45 percent of that which has been promised or committed, and much of it has taken excessively long to appear. The same is true of aid from Arab and Islamic multilateral funds, though these disbursed more of their commitments (59 percent for 1974 and 1975) than was the case for bilateral flows. Above all, for the African countries, Arab aid in all forms has covered less than 30 percent of the additional financing requirements attributable directly or indirectly to the OPEC price revolution (*Petroleum Intelligence Weekly*, 1976; Morgan Guaranty Trust, 1976; MEED, 7/3/77:39).

• Notwithstanding official declarations to the contrary, the Arab image in Africa, already historically ambiguous, appears to have suffered in the light of developments since 1973. Not only have African newspapers (most of them officially controlled) increasingly taken the oil-producing Arab states to task, but even Arab publications occasionally admit the existence of a poor Arab image in Africa. In a recent, highly revealing article published in Cairo's *Al-Siyaseh Al-Dawliyah*, a prominent academic who had returned from a ten-country African lecture tour reported widespread dissatisfaction with the scope, quality, and impact of Arab-African cooperation. The author, the dean of Cairo University's Faculty of Communications, indicated that Africans faulted Arab performance in delivering aid, criticized the Arabs for refusing to sell them oil at lower prices, and pointed out—as they saw it—that most of the Arab's vast capital accumulations were deposited in "rich countries' banks" or invested in their industries—rather than in the Third World—or spent "on extravagant luxuries" (Awdah, 1975). Other evidence suggests that these attitudes are widely held in African elite circles, though it is rare that they are officially and publicly aired.

In addition, excessive pressures on African states to vote the Arab line at international meetings and organizations has generated some resentment, as has Libya's indiscriminate support for Idi Amin and Arab aid to secessionist Eritrean forces in (African) Ethiopia. (See Chapter 7 for a discussion of other points of Arab-African conflict.) Given the cumulative effect of worsening relations between the African and Arab states, it is hardly surprising that Israeli stock appears to have gone up on the continent. The refusal of the 1975 OAU Summit in Kampala to approve an Arab resolution calling for the expulsion of Israel from the UN; the fact that two African states voted "No," and fifteen abstained, on the "Zionism-equals-racism" resolution at the UN; the open collusion between Israel and Kenya during the Entebbe raid; and the increase in Israel trade with Africa during 1975, 1976, and 1977: all suggest—at the very least—a new African flexibility on Middle East questions.[6]

Finally, probably the most important reason for the recent deterioration of Arab-African relations has been the fact that the oil-rich Arab states have begun to act, not as part of the oppressed and underprivileged part of the world, but as new members of the industrialized, imperial First World they have long denounced. Their use of petrodollar surpluses leaves little room for doubt that the Arabs' new shift is well under way. Table 2 provides a breakdown for the years 1974 to 1977, but note that the figures in Table 2 represent only investment of petrodollar surpluses; they do not cover (but are a part of) the use of petrodollar reserves, which are almost certainly much larger than those reported to the IMF, the Bank for International Settlements, or other international financial institutions. For example, if Saudi Arabia's official holdings are added to family assets, the full amount could be more than double the estimated $50 billion in state external assets (MEED, 25/3/77:46). The figures do reveal continued and relatively steady financial flows to the United States (in particular, to property and corporate equities—the "Other" category—and to long-term government securities), as well as large flows to longer-term investments in the Euromarket ("Other Countries" and U.K. "Foreign currency deposits" categories). Add to all this other growing Arab investments in Europe, North America, and even South Africa (*Interdependent*, 1976:1, 7),

TABLE 2
INVESTMENT OF "PETRODOLLAR" SURPLUSES, ESTIMATEDc
(In billions US $; percentages of totals in Parentheses)

	1974		1975		1976		1977	
UNITED KINGDOM								
Government bonds and stocks	0.9	(1.6)	0.4	(1.1)	0.2	(0.55)	0.2	(0.6)
Treasury Bills	2.7	(4.7)	-0.9	(---)	-1.2	(---)	-0.2	(---)
Sterling deposits	1.7	(3.0)	0.2	(0.6)	-1.4	(---)	0.3	(0.9)
Other Sterling Investmentsa	0.7	(1.2)	0.3	(0.8)	0.5	(1.4)	0.4	(1.2)
Foreign currency deposits	13.8	(24.2)	4.1	(11.5)	5.6	(15.6)	3.4	(10.3)
Other Foreign currency borrowings	1.2	(2.1)	0.2	(0.6)	0.8	(2.2)	---	(---)
Sub-Total	21.0	(36.8)	4.3	(12.0)	4.5	(12.6)	4.1	(12.4)
UNITED STATES								
Treasury bonds and notes	0.2	(3.5)	2.0	(5.6)	4.2	(11.7)	4.3	(13.0)
Treasury bills	5.3	(9.3)	0.5	(1.4)	-1.0	(---)	-0.8	(---)
Bank deposits	4.0	(7.0)	0.6	(1.7)	1.6	(4.5)	0.4	(1.2)
Othera	2.1	(3.7)	6.9	(19.3)	7.2	(20.1)	5.0	(15.15)
Sub-Total	11.6	(20.35)	10.0	(28.0)	12.0	(33.5)	8.9	(26.7)
OTHER COUNTRIES								
Bank deposits	9.0	(15.8)	5.0	(14.0)	7.0	(19.5)	8.5	(25.75)
Special bilateral facilities and other investmentsb	11.9	(20.9)	12.4	(34.7)	10.3	(28.8)	11.2	(33.9)
Sub-Total	20.9	(36.7)	17.4	(48.7)	17.3	(48.3)	19.7	(59.7)
INTERNATIONAL ORGANIZATIONS	3.5	(6.1)	4.0	(11.2)	2.0	(5.6)	0.3	(0.9)
Totals	57.0		35.7		35.8		33.0	
OPEC ARAB COUNTRIES & IRAN AS								
% OF TOTALS	(76.4)		(91.5)		(91.6)		(90.0)	

NOTES: a. Including equities and property
        b. Including loans to developing countries and holdings of property and equities
        c. Estimates vary; for example, the Bank of International Settlements' 46th Annual Report (Basle, 1976: 73), gives the
            1974 "Investible Surplus" as $56.9 billion, the 1975 surplus as $32.1 billion. Differences are accounted for by
            the fact that the OPEC countries themselves either give no hard figures on the subject, or if they do, provide them
            hesitatingly and often ambiguously.

SOURCES: Bank of England Quarterly Bulletin 17, 1 (March 1977): 23, and 18, 1 (March 1978):29. The adaptations and extra
          computations are ours.

plus such indications as the Saudis' reluctance to pay a promised $5 billion into the IMF's special "balance-of-payments facility" and OPEC's recent purchase of approximately 17.6 percent of the World Bank's debt (MEED, 11/2/77: 28), and the Arab transformation becomes even more obvious. To be sure, although OPEC grants and loans to developing countries absorbed some 4.5 percent of the total *reported* surplus in 1974, 12.6 percent in 1975, and 16.8 percent in 1976 (Morgan Guaranty Trust, 1976), our analysis has demonstrated that, given the direction and uses of this aid, the Arabs' disposition to treat their African allies as poor relatives was only reinforced thereby.

In sum, the evidence points to a fundamental change in both Arab behavior and in the international system of status and power. This change and its implications are discussed in Chapter 6, but of more immediate importance is consideration of the manner in which the plight of the African MSAs found responses in various international arenas and the question of the specific impact of the oil crisis on the African countries themselves. It is to this latter problem that we turn next.

3

The Economic Consequences
of the 1973-74 Oil Crisis
on African Countries

It is very much easier to describe the political impact of the
1973-74 Middle East crisis—and the revolution of petroleum
pricing—upon the non-Arab African states than it is to assess
the economic consequences of these same events. Chapter 2
summarized such political responses as the official severance
of diplomatic and aid links with Israel, shifts in voting patterns
in various international forums, and Arab and African
diplomatic initiatives, and then suggested a pattern of African
disillusionment leading to increased Arab-African estrange-
ment. In the same chapter, the beginnings of a pattern of Arab-
African cooperation, largely compensatory, was also noted,
and in subsequent chapters the response of a number of key
international bodies and institutions to the post-1973 situation
will be described. Basic to our argument has been the
contention that the more recent political reactions of the
African states, as manifested in the growing rift between them
and their Arab allies and in their initiatives to and within
international institutions, flow in large measure from what the
Africans claim were—and are—economic dislocations caused
in part or mainly by the crises of 1973-74. These difficulties,
African leaders have argued, were insufficiently appreciated by
the Arabs, and thus Arab responses, while generous, still fell—
and fall—largely short of the Africans' real needs.

Spokesmen for the Arabs, at the Afro-Arab Summit in 1977
and elsewhere, have argued that (1) they, the Arabs, have been
more than generous in meeting the obligation to shield their
friends from the most destructive effects of the 1973-74

economic crises; (2) the Africans have failed to appreciate the Arabs' own developmental imperatives; (3) the Africans have been unable to agree about their priorities and appear to be unwilling to impose the necessary institutional self-discipline to make the best use of that which has been offered them; (4) the impact on African economies has been greatly exaggerated and, in any case, requires well-planned and well-differentiated responses; and (5) such economic difficulties as were experienced by African states after 1973 were caused not by higher oil prices but by massive inflation in the West, which then translated into a "continual deterioration in the terms of trade between underdeveloped and industrialized countries" (Asfahany, 1977:29; the argument is summarized by Legum, 1976:A76-A80 and in Legum, 1977:A96-A107).

The nub of the dispute, of course, is not in a disagreement about whether the crises did or did not have negative economic consequences for the African non-oil-producing countries—it is generally conceded that they did—but in questions about the sorts of consequences, how much weight to assign to the oil crisis, and the extent of Arab obligations to those affected. The African position is clearly based on the contention that Arab obligations are linked both to promises of compensation and to sets of very real difficulties encountered by African economies after 1973. The Arab position is that their obligations are limited because the damage was not of their doing, was limited in any case, and because they were not responsible for the Africans' overblown expectations of Arab compensation.

It becomes useful, therefore, to try to come to grips with such substance as there is in the shadowy problem of economic consequences, since it then may be possible to suggest the extent to which more purely political considerations have come to affect the Arab-African relationship.

Insofar as there is consensus among those who comment on the subject, it is agreed that the 1973-74 oil crisis directly affected African economies in three general areas. (1) Import bills for oil rose precipitately for the African non-oil-producing countries. The exact amounts are variously estimated from a low $650-$750 million (Lottem, 1977:10) to approximately $1.2 billion (Bustros, 1978:94) as against approximately $300 million in 1973. (2) Foreign currency and other international reserves of the non-oil developing countries (NODCs) were seriously depleted to meet the increased costs of oil and petrochemicals (Asfahany, 1977:29). (3) The NODCs experienced balance-of-payments strains ranging from declines in favorable balances to aggravated deficits, all depending on the countries' abilities to adjust to the crisis (Yaori, 1974; *Development Forum*, 1978; Chibwe, 1976; Erb and Low, 1977; Low, 1974; Lottem, 1977; Bustros, 1978; Asfahany, 1977; Bobrow, Kurdle, and Pirages, 1977). Indirect consequences included (1) significantly higher import bills for industrial and other products from the West, without marked increases in import volumes; (2) vastly increased borrowing from bilateral and multilateral sources, resulting in much higher external debts and, therefore, higher debt service payments; (3) various internal dislocations ranging from deferred or disrupted development programs, to production shortfalls, to accelerated internal inflation with its attendant effects on standards of living. Overall, the estimates offered by the World Bank (IBRD, 1976)—that some thirty-nine LDCs paid roughly $9.7 billion more for oil and $5 billion more for fertilizers in 1974 than they did in 1973—are taken seriously by most observers and confirmed in their reports (Krapels, 1977; Bustros, 1978; Erb and Low, 1977:213-14). In a related development on a broader plane, the balance-of-payments picture for the world's NODCs, including the African MSAs, became quite bleak. According to the Bank of International Settlements, the aggregate current-account deficit of the NODCs is estimated to have risen between 1974 and 1975 from $15 billion to $25 billion, not including LDCs' receipts from unofficial unilateral transfers, but "the combined deficit of these countries may be estimated as having gone up from $23 milliard [billion] in 1974 to $36 milliard [billion] in 1975" (BIS, 1976:74). Most of the deficit seems to have been covered by borrowings, but, for the group, official reserves still fell by approximately $2 billion in thie period. Erb and Low argue that

For the low-income countries designated by the United Nations as "most seriously affected" (MSA) by the crisis, the payments gap which had to be met by emergency measures amounted to over $3.1 billion in 1974. By mid-1975 the original group of thirty-two had been increased to forty-two and would have been still larger if a cut-off level of $400 per capita had not been applied. The shortfall in 1975 beyond their regular capital inflows was estimated at $4.4 billion, of which emergency assistance covered $1.5 billion (1977:214).

Narrowing the focus still further and extending the period covered, the aggregate data on payments balances for all forty-seven African NODCs provide additional support for these contentions. According to the United Nations Conference on Trade and Development figures published in 1977, the net current-account balances for the forty-seven countries were projected at minus $9.1 billion by the end of 1978, compared to minus $2.2 billion in 1973, despite recent small decreases in the trade and reserves deficits and substantial increases in net capital flows (UNCTAD, 1977:43).

If there is consensus on the general situation, there is much less agreement on the details, both with respect to the several factors involved and upon their specific impact on particular African economies. The difficulty appears to be the classic one of attempting to isolate the effects of a single factor—even one as visible as increases up to 400 percent in the price of a vital commodity—upon an economy. Without going into a detailed discussion of the problem, it can be asserted that the task is virtually an impossible one and the results from such exercises are almost always likely to suffer from serious defects. At the minimum, for example, the *ceteris paribus* assumptions that must be made can seldom be sustained realistically in longitudinal analysis, the only way by which results have much operational meaning. Moreover, that which appears as a reasonable conclusion from aggregate analysis may be considerably less so when the data are broken down by country.

An example in point is the highly interesting and useful attempt to assess the short-term consequences of expensive oil—viewed as a "contrived scarcity"—by Bobrow, Kurdle and

Pirages. Using accepted techniques of multivariate analysis coupled to regression equations, the authors sought to measure the impact of expensive oil on the net growth rates of some seventy countries, divided into "industrial," "developing," and "less developed" categories. The thirty-eight-country "less developed" subsample was obtained by excluding states with less than one million in population or $100 million GNP, or for which data were unreliable, and it included all the African states they used (nineteen, including Egypt, Tunisia, Morocco, and Sudan). We will not review their analysis in detail, but some of their results are interesting: the "industrial" countries were the hardest hit and suffered the greatest deflections from pre-1974 growth rates; the "developing" group was the next hardest hit and, of the three, least able to adjust to the price increases; and the "less developed" subsample suffered the smallest average deflection (1977:632-34). More specifically, the thirty-eight "less developed" (including seventeen of the nineteen African) states that were neither fuel nor nonfuel mineral exporters experienced almost no downward deflection in their growth rates in 1974, and an aggregate downward deflection of only .4 percent in 1975 (1977:634). The authors conclude that dire predictions about the effects of the OPEC oil crisis upon the poorer countries—including the African—appear to have been exaggerated. On its face, the analysis is suitably cautious, careful, and respectful of exceptions and awkward marginals; its conclusions are eminently reasonable as well. Most African states use little oil: overall, African NODCs consumed only approximately fifteen million tons in 1973, and most of them were quickly able to find offsetting finance from such sources as their own reserves, OPEC, the Common Market, Franc Zone transfers (if they were ex–French colonies), the IMF, etc.

The difficulty, for us, is that the authors' subsample—justified by their criteria—did not include most smaller African countries and, in fact, left out some that clearly fell within their criteria for inclusion: Guinea, Mauritania, Cameroon, Congo/Brazzaville. In fact, had they focused only on African "less developed" countries and included all non-Arab and non-OPEC states independent in 1973 (thirty-one, without Rhodesia and South Africa), their conclusions would have had to be modified. Using their techniques and our augmented African subsample, we estimate that the African group had an aggregate, average downward deflection of 2.3 percent in 1974 and 3.1 percent in 1975. A truism of economic growth analysis is that all growth is not equivalent; the same rate of growth in a strong and in a weak economy will have different consequences and meanings for the economies concerned. Thus the African deflections—lower in fact than some experienced in the industrialized countries—may in fact represent much more serious economic difficulties than in the industrialized group, which managed to rebound relatively soon after their difficulties in 1974-75. Even that modest revision, because it is based on an aggregate statistic, conceals important differences of impact between various African states and for the group as a whole. These can be examined briefly with an analysis using a modified version of the "consensual rubrics" noted earlier.

Of a number of possible indicators of oil-price impact on individual African economies, at least four were highly visible and readily documented: (1) changes in foreign-reserves positions, (2) increases in imported oil bills, (3) changes in total CIF (cost, insurance, and freight) import bills, and (4) changes in the relationship between oil import bills and the CIF import bills. The logic in choosing these indicators involves not only the fact that they are among those most frequently cited in arguments about the short-term impact of increased oil prices, but also because they have the added utility of condensing other impact factors as well. For example, indicators (3) and (4), which use CIF rather than FOB (freight on board) import figures, include the higher costs of transport attributable to the oil-price increases themselves, and indicator (4) subsumes the effect of inflated prices paid for products bought from industrialized countries.

In our analysis, we used a representative ten-country oil consumption sample ranging from Kenya, Black Africa's highest NODC consumer, to two of the continent's lowest consumers, Burundi and The Gambia. Our base was also 1973. We included countries with substantial development (Kenya, Ivory Coast), some that were very poor by almost all indices

(Burundi, The Gambia, Ethiopia), some that were also hurt by the great drought of 1973-75 (Senegal, Niger, Tanzania, Ethopia), and some showing only modest growth (Malawi, Madagascar, Senegal).

The results of our analysis, and the changes in order of rank according to each indicator, are summarized in Table 3. Briefly stated, the conclusions that can be drawn from this analysis, and later data, tend to confirm the general picture previously drawn from the aggregate data. These conclusions also highlight some important differences between individual African countries as well as between groups of African states distinguished according to some of the criteria we used in selecting our consumption sample. Predictably, for indicators (2) through (4) the high consumers, who also tend to be countries with comparatively high development levels, suffered the most severe short-term effects. What was not predictable was the scale of the impact. The Ivory Coast's 1974 bill for imported oil went up by 440 percent over its 1973 level; Kenya's, by 317 percent; and in both cases, even increased during the following two years. In both economies, the share of petroleum imports as a percentage of total CIF imports also increased precipitately. It more than doubled in Kenya, from 7.6 percent in 1973 to 18.6 percent in 1974, and almost trebled in the Ivory Coast, from 3.6 percent in 1973 to 13.4 percent in 1974. Tanzania, a relatively high consumer, ranked near or at the top of all four indicator lists. Tanzania's problems with imported oil were compounded by other difficulties, notably drought, which drastically lowered food production and forced an increase in the food import bill from 274 million shillings (U.S. $39 million) in 1973 to over one billion shillings (U.S. $140 million) in 1974. Despite massive borrowing from abroad—for example, $217.7 million from the IMF Oil Facility between 1974 and 1977, which helped improve its reserve position from $50 million in 1973 to $281.8 in 1977—and despite the compensatory effects of substantial increases in the volumes and unit value of its principal exports during 1975 and 1976 (coffee, 127 to 318; cotton, 191 to 313), its economy continued in trouble through 1977. At the end of 1976, oil imports still accounted for 14.7 percent of Tanzania's total CIF imports

TABLE 3

FOUR IMPACT INDICATORS OF 1973-74 OIL CRISIS AND COMPARATIVE

RANKINGS FOR AN AFRICAN CONSUMPTION SAMPLE

(1) CHANGES IN INTERNATIONAL RESERVES STATUS 1973-74, PERCENTAGES

1.	Tanzania	- 188.0
2.	Senegal	- 90.4
3.	Malawi	- 60.6
4.	Madagascar	- 37.4
5.	Burundi	- 31.1
6.	Ivory Coast	- 25.5
7.	Kenya	- 17.1
8.	Niger	- 10.2
9.	Ethiopia	+ 55.6
10.	Gambia	+ 78.6

(2) INCREASES IN NET OIL BILLS 1973-74, PERCENTAGES

1.	Ivory Coast	440.0
2.	Kenya	317.0
3.	Tanzania	280.0
4.	Madagascar	224.0
5.	Senegal	196.8
6.	Ethiopia	142.1
7.	Niger	111.0
8.	Gambia	88.0
9.	Malawi	23.0
10.	Burundi	18.3

(3) INCREASES IN TOTAL CIF IMPORT BILLS 1973-74, PERCENTAGES

1.	Ivory Coast	74.7
2.	Kenya	69.7
3.	Tanzania	54.0
4.	Senegal	49.0
5.	Madagascar	49.0
6.	Malawi	41.0
7.	Burundi	36.0
8.	Ethiopia	31.7
9.	Gambia	30.4
10.	Niger	21.0

(4) OIL IMPORTS AS % OF TOTAL CIF IMPORT BILLS, 1973 AND 1974

		(1973)	(1974)
1.	Ivory Coast	3.6	13.4
2.	Kenya	7.6	18.6
3.	Madagascar	7.3	16.0
4.	Senegal	5.8	11.7
5.	Tanzania	9.7	18.6
6.	Ethiopia	9.3	17.2
7.	Niger	7.8	13.6
8.	Gambia	5.3	7.0
9.	Malawi	6.5	8.0
10.	Burundi	5.1	6.1

1973 CONSUMPTION SAMPLE (in millions tons p.a.)

1.	Kenya	2.10
2.	Ivory Coast	1.40
3.	Tanzania	.90
4.	Madagascar	.85
5.	Senegal	.85
6.	Ethiopia	.80
7.	Malawi	.20
8.	Niger	.10
9.	Burundi	.03
10.	Gambia	.03

CONSUMPTION SAMPLE RE-RANKED, MOST TO LEAST AFFECTED (SUM, INDICATOR RANKS)

1.	Ivory Coast
2.	Tanzania
3.	Kenya
4.	Senegal
5.	Madagascar
6.	Malawi
7.	Ethiopia
8.	Niger
9.	Burundi
10.	Gambia

Sources: IMF, International Financial Statistics, March, 1978.
           International Petroleum Encyclopedia, 1974.

(compared to 9.7 percent in 1973), down from a high of 18.6 percent in 1974 (**IBRD**, 1977:72-74).

Overall, it should be noted that even though fortuitously higher prices for key export commodities might have helped cushion the impact of higher oil prices (coffee: Tanzania,

Madagascar, Kenya, Burundi, Ethiopia, Ivory Coast; cocoa: Ivory Coast; groundnuts: The Gambia, Senegal), these increases either came too late—coffee, in 1976—to help overcome the initial crunch or were insufficient to offset such indirect effects as the massive increase in the import prices of products from the industrialized countries.

Also predictably, the low consumers suffered the lowest initial damage from the oil crisis. This group includes not only Burundi and The Gambia, but also Guinea-Bissau, Equatorial Guinea, Upper Volta, and Rwanda—which consumed .04, .05, .06, and .04 million tons per annum, respectively, in 1973. Most of these countries are quite poor, with small or almost nonexistent export sectors, and consequently were able to weather the crisis with less damage to their economies than in the case of the high consumers whose expanding economies relied heavily on increased oil imports to help fuel their economic growth. There were two special cases: Burundi, which, despite some initial problems, found some compensation in higher prices for its coffee; and The Gambia, which found immediate help from higher 1974 prices for groundnuts, enabling it to double its export income with only a modest increase in production volume.

Our first indicator, changes in international reserves status, is one of the better indicators of initial impact and the least reliable in assessing long-term effects. The problem is that while most African countries dipped heavily into their reserves to help relieve their initial payments imbalances, almost all managed not only to replenish their reserves within two or three years but to increase them substantially—in our sample, all except Madagascar had done both by 1977. To some extent, as we indicated earlier, this change was due to the effect of fortuitously higher prices for such commodities as cocoa, coffee, and groundnuts, or, in the case of Niger, to an oil-crisis-related jump in the price of uranium ore. It was also due to substantial compensatory transfers from Western, international, and, to a lesser extent, Arab sources to the MSAs. However, the change did not also necessarily indicate that all the economies concerned had fully recovered from the oil crisis or that they had regained their developmental momentum.

Tanzania is a case in point: although its international reserves rose to $87.7 million in 1977, $21.1 million over 1973, by the end of 1977 it remained heavily in debt to those who helped it between 1974 and 1976 with domestic savings and capitalization still at or below 1973 levels, and it was forced to readjust its socialist developmental goals and priorities. Ghana is another good illustration. By 1977 its reserves had almost reached 1973 levels, and, like the Ivory Coast, it benefited from a cocoa price bonanza. However, a compound of high, initial oil crisis impact (for example, a minus 101.4 percent change in its reserves position), pervasive economic mismanagement, galloping inflation, and political uncertainty all contributed to an economic decline that by June 1978 had brought the Ghanian economy to the edge of disaster. The examples could be multiplied, but our point would remain the same: some African countries appear to have weathered the initial impact of the oil crisis and, like the Ivory Coast, Cameroon, and Niger, have regained their growth momentum. Still others have found their recovery stymied or short-circuited by exogenous factors bearing little relationship to oil or oil prices. Political instability in Ethiopia, Mauritania, Uganda, Chad, Congo/Brazzaville, Zaire, Equatorial Guinea, and Guinea, among other countries, has had this effect, as did the sharp decreases in the world market price of copper for Zambia and the aftereffects of the 1973-75 drought for Chad, Mali, Upper Volta, Ethiopia, and Tanzania.

On the whole, however, there is little question that the direct, indirect, and multiplier effects of the oil crisis have strained all non-Arab African economies except the fortunate OPEC members—Nigeria and Gabon—or those countries that, like Niger, produce an energy-related commodity such as uranium. Several economies, such as those of Kenya and Tanzania, have either been damaged severely or have taken longer to recover than their more advantaged neighbors. In general, and taking into consideration other factors such as those noted above, the oil crisis was directly related to accelerated inflation, higher foreign indebtedness, and disrupted development plans in most African countries. It is highly probable, therefore, that at the base of African discontent with the Arab-African relationship there lies not so much a set of objective and easily identifiable effects on particular countries, but a much more diffuse—but we think correct—perception that Africa's other difficulties were compounded by the effects of the oil crisis.

It may well be true, as some Arab spokesmen have charged, that the African reaction to the oil crisis was all out of proportion to its actual impact on African economies. For the Africans, that is hardly the point. Their discomfort was very real, and all the more so because of the pattern of expectations created during the 1967-73 period of Arab-African rapprochement. As was noted earlier, the beginnings of African disillusion with the relationship found political voice as early as 1974. The consequences described above gave substance to that voice, and, more recently, points of aggravated conflict between African and Arab states, which will be discussed in our final chapter, have added angry overtones to it as well.

4

The Response of International Aid Institutions

The hardest-hit victims of OPEC's unilateral oil-price hikes undoubtedly were the least and less developed countries of the so-called Third World. Although 70 percent self-sufficient in their energy usage, the remaining 30 percent of their energy needs is accounted for almost exclusively by imported oil. For these countries, in 1974 the cost of OPEC oil imports alone increased by nearly $12 billion to a level of almost $17 billion (OECD, 1975:37). The increased oil bills of the African MSAs reached overwhelming levels: Sierra Leone's oil bill rose 270 percent from 1973 to 1974, Tanzania's oil payments rose 280 percent from 1973 to 1974, and Zambia's oil costs increased 165 percent during the same period (*Afro-Asian Affairs*, 1975). Unable to wrest concessionary prices from OPEC, the Third and Fourth World countries either went further into public debt, spent their scarce foreign-exchange reserves, or instituted strict new import controls along with price regulation to meet their high energy bills. Many of the higher-income Third World countries were able to recover somewhat by expanding export earnings; however, the African MSA nations were left with only one basic alternative—to seek new, special international relief funds.

Although largely preoccupied with their own oil-price raises, the OECD states and the international aid structures tied to them contrived a variety of ad hoc arrangements to lessen the impact of the price rise on the forty-two MSAs, twenty-seven of which were African states. Similarly, fearing for their position of "moral leaders" in the Third World, the Arab and other

OPEC states, as was noted earlier, created several new bilateral and multilateral aid payment schemes. In addition, states with some economic collateral who sought to cope with higher import prices—such as Kenya, Zaire, and Zambia—drew extensively upon commercial banks dealing in the Euro-currency market. Plainly, the international aid flows of the post-1973/1974 period are much different than those of the years leading up to 1973. The aid disbursements by the Development Assistance Committee (DAC) of OECD have doubled in the past ten years, but disbursements by multilateral aid organizations have increased sixfold in the same period of time (OECD, 1976:103). In real terms, DAC area aid is down 10 percent from 1966; still, 1974 and 1975 witnessed new efforts to raise assistance levels as DAC aid rose from $9.4 billion in 1973 to $13.6 billion in 1975 (OECD, 1976:16). OPEC aid commitments, although slow in disbursements, rose from $1.5 billion in 1973 to $9 billion in 1975 (OECD, 1976:100). A Chase Manhattan Bank research study reported that Arab oil producers had dispensed $19,000 million in soft loans and grants from 1973 to 1978—$16,000 million were distributed by Saudi Arabia, Kuwait, and the UAE, United Arab Emirates (MEED, 4/14/78:15). Moreover, the international private banks have vastly increased their lending activities to the NODCs. In 1968-72, annual private-bank lending to the LDCs averaged $1 billion, but in 1975 lending skyrocketed to $7.6 billion (OECD, 1976:39). Still, the main effect of the 1973 oil-price hike, namely, the transfer of over $100 billion worldwide, $10 billion of it from among the NODCs, to the OPEC states' treasuries, has yet to be fully compensated for by intergovern-mental, multilateral, or private banking schemes of development assistance (Cleveland and Brittain, 1977:740).

Clearly, the OECD DAC countries' response to the oil-price crisis remained circumscribed by the serious effects of the 1974-75 recession. While the OPEC oil hikes deeply eroded the NODCs' current-account balances in 1973 and 1974, the general economic slowdown in the OECD area and its resultant lowering of trade caused a current-accounts deficit of $21.5 billion in 1974, $32.5 billion in 1975, and $24 billion in 1976 (*Banker*, 1977:92). Indeed, the loss in NODC-OECD trade in

1974 alone was equal to the NODCs' loss in increased 1974 oil prices (OECD, 1975:39-40). In reaction to their own economic doldrums, the OECD nations tightened Eurocurrency lending to the NODCs, applied higher credit-worthiness standards to NODC borrowers, decreased levels of foreign investment except in nations with energy potential, and experienced less demand for NODC exports. Forced themselves to draw upon IMF borrowing and special bilateral aid arrangements—as in Italy's $2 billion loan from West Germany in 1974 and the United Kingdom's $3.9 billion IMF loan in 1976—the OECD states opted for increased international trade as the best means to revive the NODCs' injured economies.

Yet this policy of increasing NODC export earning through expanded trade with the OECD nations had little impact on the African MSA economies whose export earnings, marketing networks, and structural development do not respond well to simply increasing trade. The "Trade Pledge," adopted in May 1974 and renewed in May 1975, forestalled trade restrictions and artificial stimulation of exports, and tightened current-accounts transactions within the OECD area with some positive effect on the NODC economies tied into this import market. Still, beyond this long-run trade strategy, the OECD DAC countries reacted to the hardships of the MSA NODCs with a succession of short-term aid payment structures.

The existing international aid and development institutions reacted by forming ad hoc adjunct programs within their already operating programs. The IMF proved especially important as a credit source for the MSA African states, although much of its resources remain monopolized by the badly off OECD states such as the United Kingdom and Italy. The IMF chartered its special Oil Facility in 1974, borrowing 3 billion in SDRs (mainly from OPEC reserves) to aid all oil-pressed nations. The 1974 drawings on the Oil Facility amounted to 2.6 billion SDRs; yet, only 40 percent of this sum went to the NODCs as European nations like the United Kingdom, Portugal, and Italy fought to stay afloat economically (OECD, 1975:46). Renewed in January 1975 and authorized to borrow up to 5 billion more SDRs, the IMF special Oil Facility—also known as the Witteveen facility—

loaned 505 million SDRs to the NODCs up to August of 1975. A special subsidy account was also activated to reduce the effective interest rate paid by the MSA countries by five percentage points, and by September 1975 nearly half of a 312-million SDR account set aside for that purpose had been utilized (OECD, 1975:46).

Unfortunately, a new $16 billion "Witteveen facility" on the drawing boards since late 1975 has encountered difficulty in raising capital subscriptions and in determining its aid targets. Intended to draw Saudi Arabia "into the higher councils of international finance" (MEED, 4/22/77:22), the new facility aimed at raising $4.8 billion from Saudi Arabia as well as additional OPEC contributions which would be equally matched by the OECD nations (MEED, 5/6/77:13). The OPEC states demand that the new fund be earmarked exclusively for use by the NODCs, but this requirement has been resisted by the OECD states who seek access to the new moneys for themselves. Hence, the OECD's stipulations for open access and questions over Saudi Arabia's ability to subscribe even $4 billion to the facility have left its future undetermined. Nevertheless, the initial special Oil Facility provided significant assistance to the African MSAs during the worst months of the oil-price crisis.

At the World Bank (IBRD), the International Development Agency (IDA), along with the EEC nations, committed $376 million in nonproject assistance to the MSA countries during 1974. Yet, unable to meet fully the needs of the MSA borrowers, the IBRD opened the "Third Window" lending funds from its $1 billion reserve at 4 percent rates in July 1975. Ultimately, contributions rose to $117 million enabling the IBRD to let out over $500 million loans from the "Third Window" (OECD, 1975:23). At the same time, much of the IBRD's new lending was concentrated in Africa with $424.2 million in loans during 1975—a 50 percent increase over 1974 and a 139 percent increase over the 1969-73 yearly average (*African Development*, 1975:23). Moreover, much of this new lending reflected the IBRD's new interest in rural development and agricultural modernization among the MSA countries of Africa as such projects garnered 57 percent of all loans in 1974 and 1975 compared to 17 percent yearly averages during 1969-73 (*African Development*, 1975:23).

Still, the poorest 40 percent of the rural population in the MSAs usually receives no direct benefits from international loans such as those of the IBRD (MEED, 4/22/77:10). Hence, in November 1974 the World Food Conference proposed the formation of the International Fund for Agricultural Development (IFAD), which by December 1976 had raised $1 billion in pledges for new loans. The OECD DAC countries responded by pledging $567.3 million to the IFAD as the OPEC states gave $435.5 million (MEED, 4/22/77:9). Recognizing the inefficiency of the conventional aid pipelines, the OECD states backed the IFAD to insure help for "the poorest people in the poorest countries" (MEED, 4/22/77:10). Most of the funds will be lent at extremely soft terms: fifty-year loans at 1 percent interest. A clear victory for the MSA countries which rely so heavily upon their traditional agricultural sectors, the IFAD also represents another avenue of OPEC influence as many of the non-oil Islamic developing states are expected to be the IFAD's first customers.

Other short-term OECD assistance was given to the MSA countries through the United Nations Emergency Operation (UNEO) established by the Sixth Special Session of the United Nations general assembly in May 1974. A special account at the disposal of the Secretary General pooled $280 million for this MSA-oriented fund. Sixty percent of the money was solicited from the OPEC states and the remainder from the OECD DAC countries, mainly from within the EEC (OECD, 1975:46). Furthermore, the OECD nations scraped together a variety of short-run, nonproject funds for disbursement through bilateral and multilateral channels. Over $1 billion was distributed in 1974, $750 million through bilateral channels and $250 million through multilateral agencies; while another $.7 billion in such funding was committed but not delivered in 1974 (OECD, 1975:45-46).

The OPEC countries' response to the oil-price crisis was immediate and generous, but, at the same time, very unevenly distributed. OPEC aid to Arab states represented 59.6 percent of its total aid in 1974, which dropped to 40.4 percent in 1977, while aid to non-Arab African countries rose to 34 percent of total OPEC aid only in 1977 (MEED, 4/14/78:15). Like the OECD DAC nations, the OPEC states worked through existing multilateral channels of international assistance and they opened their own bilateral avenues of aid distribution. Moreover, the extent of their new financial resources was such that the Arab OPEC states organized several new multilateral structures for disbursing aid among the African and Asian NODCs. While mainly oriented toward aiding the non-oil Islamic states, the Arab OPEC countries also greatly assisted the EEC nations with loans, grants, and new investment during the 1974-75 recession.

Prior to the 1973 oil-price crisis, the Arab OPEC countries maintained only two international aid institutions. The Arab Fund for Economic and Social Development (AFESD), founded in May 1968 for financing joint international projects involving more than one Arab nation, has present capital assets of $347 million (*Arab Economist*, 1977:38). The second agency, the Arab-African Technical Assistance Fund (ATAFA), was established in December 1973, in the midst of the oil-price increase, as a symbolic gesture to Arab-African solidarity. Its essentially "symbolic" function is signaled by its minute assets, $25 million, and the long lag in its beginning to give aid— authorized in December 1973 and opening twenty months later in August 1975 (*Arab Economist*, 1977:40). To sustain their international legitimacy as "moral spokesmen" for the Third and Fourth Worlds, the Arab states of OPEC turned to existing international institutions, such as the agencies of the Arab League, OAPEC, and OPEC, to construct new aid delivery systems for the NODCs.

"To reinforce economic, financial and technical cooperation between the African and Arab countries" (*Arab Economist*, 1977:38), the Arab OPEC states chartered the Arab Bank for Economic Development in Africa (BADEA) in November 1973, but the doors did not actually open until January 1975. With funds targeted exclusively for non-Arab African countries, the BADEA is the only Arab-African multilateral institution for Arab aid in sub-Saharan Africa. Initially funded with $231 million, the BADEA cofinances its projects with the IBRD, the

African Development Bank, the Arab Fund, or OECD DAC nations. Although much smaller than the Islamic Development ment Bank, the BADEA authorized twelve loans in 1975 for a total commitment of $85.5 million; in 1976, the BADEA loaned $57.5 million in a total of nine loans up to June (OECD, 1976:110). By February 1977, the BADEA had disbursed over $143 million to twenty projects throughout Africa (MEED, 3/4/77:7), and in March 1977 secured an additional pledge of $160 million from Saudi Arabia, Kuwait, and the UAE (MEED, 3/1/77:9). To be sure, these moneys provided a welcome new source of relief to Africa's MSA economies; still, the BADEA's efforts were basically only a drop in the bucket. Kenya's increased oil bills in 1975 alone came to $215 million, $169 million more than 1973; yet, the BADEA's total aid delivery for *all* of Africa in 1975 was only $86 million (MEED, 3/4/77:7).

In sharp contrast to the BADEA's small assets, the Islamic Development Bank (IDB) was set up in June 1974 to aid twenty-four Arab and Islamic countries including a number of African MSAs—Egypt, Guinea, Mali, Mauritania, and Sudan. In keeping with the Arab OPEC countries' foreign policies, this multilateral institution opened for business with $2.4 billion in capital assets, over ten times the reserves of the BADEA (*Arab Economist*, 1977:39). Although a small number of African states were eligible for business at the IDB—Algeria, Cameroon, Egypt, Guinea, Libya, Mali, Mauritania, Morocco, Nigeria, Senegal, Sudan, and Tunisia—the bulk of its assistance was earmarked for the Arab "frontline" states, the Arab OPEC countries themselves, and the Asian MSAs— Afghanistan, Bangladesh, Pakistan, and the two Yemeni republics (*Arab Economist*, 1977:39). By 1977, it had invested $273 million in over forty countries and was financing $50.1 million of vital imports to hard-pressed Islamic states in 1977 (MEED, 3/17/1978:17-18).

While Arab commitments to African-oriented development banks proved somewhat paltry in comparison to their financial aid to Islam, the Arab states did give special attention to the African MSAs' oil problem through the Special Arab Fund for African Oil Importers (SAFA—also known as the Afro-Arab Oil Assistance Fund). Authorized to give up to $200 million in oil-facility credits at a 1 percent interest rate, SAFA allotted $25.15 million in 1974 to eleven African states—Kenya's allotment in 1974, for instance, was $3.6 million (MEED, 3/18/77:7)—and disbursed $118 million in 1975 to twenty-seven African countries. In comparison, the OAPEC Special Account of $80 million offered interest-free loans for twenty years to five Arab MSA states. According to a programmed formula, Sudan received 48 percent of the Special Account's disbursements, the Yemen Arab Republic 18 percent, the Yemen People's Democratic Republic 14 percent, Somalia 11 percent, and Mauritania 9 percent. All loans carry a ten-year grace period which builds a 75 percent grant element into the loans (*Arab Economist,* 1977:22). In addition to the OAPEC Special Account, the Arab NODCs—like Sudan, Tunisia, Somalia, Egypt, Mauritania, and the Yemeni republics—can draw upon the Arab Monetary Fund (AMF) established in April 1977. The Fund's current capitalization is $875 million, and members may draw up to four times their national subscriptions from the AMF to handle balance-of-payments, currency value, and international trade accounts (MEED, 4/2/77:22). Most of the Arab NODCs, then, are well taken care of by the Arab OPEC states; however, the African NODCs and MSAs continue to incur oil deficits. The SAFA program was continued into 1976 and 1977, but the responsibility for its management was transferred to the BADEA in 1976.

The OPEC Special Fund was chartered in January 1976 with starting capital reserves of $800 million. Over half of this immense sum was contributed by Iran and Saudi Arabia, which proved instrumental in tagging $435.5 million as OPEC's share of the IFAD's initial reserves. The remainder of the Special Fund remains available for soft loans to NODCs with balance-of-payment problems; over $35 million in soft loans were arranged for African states by January 1977 (MEED, 3/4/1977:7). In 1977 its resources rose to $1,600.6 million, and it had committed over $477 million to various aid agencies, while receiving an additional $400 million for 1978-79 from its OPEC backers (MEED, 4/21/1978:15).

In addition to improvising these multilateral aid programs immediately after the 1973 oil-price increases, the Arab states also opened new aid options to Arab and African NODCs in their national aid structures, such as the Kuwait Fund for Arab Economic Development (KFAED), the Saudi Development Fund (SDF), the Abu Dhabi Fund for Arab Economic Development, and the External Iraq Fund for Development. The KFAED with $3.4 billion in capital assets opened in early 1974 to non-Arab NODCs to displace the impact of higher oil prices with new aid distributions (*Arab Economist*, 1977:40). Likewise, in May and June of 1974 the SDF, the Abu Dhabi Fund, and the External Iraq Fund allowed non-Arab NODCs to make loans for development projects, and the African MSAs have taken advantage of this opportunity. The Arab OPEC states have also stepped up their lending and commercial activities with the African states through the existing network of joint commercial and development banks: the Afro-Arab Bank of Cairo, the Libyan Arab Foreign Bank, the Union des Banques Arabo-Françaises, the International Arab Bank for External Trade and Development, the Kuwaiti-Senegalese Investment Bank, and the Kuwait Foreign Trading, Contracting, and Investment Company (*Arab Economist*, 1977:42-43).

Finally, as was discussed above, the OPEC countries responded to the African and Asian MSAs by contributing to joint efforts with the OECD DAC nations. Eighty-seven percent of the IMF's Oil Facility was borrowed from the OPEC states; $1.8 billion in 1974 and $2.9 billion in 1975 was disbursed by OPEC. OPEC members—Kuwait, Qatar, Saudi Arabia, the UAE, and Venezuela—committed $62 million to the IBRD's "Third Window" in 1975, and Kuwait gave $9 million to the IDA in 1975 as well (OECD, 1976:20). As the motive forces behind many of the international aid institutions' responses to the 1973 oil-price increases, the Arab OPEC countries proved to be less than perfect sources of developmental assistance. Their responses, relative to the OECD DAC nations were both immediate and generous in terms of commitments made. By 1976, the top six foreign aid donors— in terms of foreign aid as a proportion of GNP—were OPEC states. The OECD states gave an average of .33 percent of their GNP, while the OPEC states gave 2.7 percent (MEED, 12/19/1977:24). However, all too often commitments took months to become actual aid payments. The Arab OPEC states' response to the African countries' needs, by and large, was slow in coming, inadequate in amount, and sluggish in disbursement.

Yet, for the most part, the Arab and OPEC institutional reaction was enough to forestall, if not defuse, a good deal of the Africans' criticisms and to keep up the OPEC states' slippery hold on their "moral leadership" position among the NODCs. In fact, within OPEC itself, the claim to highest moral leadership also seems to be passing to the "banker" Arab states of the Gulf and away from the "industrializer" Arab OPEC nations so well known for their radicalism in the past.[7] The "industrializers'" inability to contribute sizable funds to NODC aid facilities, with the exception of Iran, and the "banker" Arab states' desire to conduct their foreign policies, at least in part, through their banks and development corporations has led to this shift as Table 4 illustrates. In both percentage of GNP terms and absolute amounts, the "banker" Arab states are far outstripping the "industrializer" states in their development aid programs. Undoubtedly, the lower aid disbursements of "radical" Algeria and Iraq are lessening their authority in Arab-African relations. The African states, as the March 1977 Cairo Summit revealed, "have turned their attention away from 'radical' Arab nations towards Gulf Arab states which they feel offer something more tangible" (MEED, 4/18/1977:7). The "tangibility" of the Gulf states' aid is reflected in Table 4. Unlike the radical "industrializers," the moderate "banker" Arab states of OPEC have the financial resources to significantly assist and back the African countries. And, as pragmatists, the African states' leaders are correctly seeking, and now finding, greener pastures for their development lobbying in the more "moderate" rather than the more "radical" Arab capitals.

The other international financial institution which reacted to the new challenge of the oil-price increase was the private banking industry, especially those banks located in the OECD nations. In fact, the international private banking industry crossed an important divide in 1974-75 as its lending patterns underwent a "major shift from developed to developing countries" (OECD, 1976:77). To be sure, most of this increased

Table 4

OPEC States' Aid Contributions to the NODCs

	(% of GNP)		(Total Millions of $)	
"Industrializers"	1974	1975	1974	1975
Algeria	.37%	.14%	$ 42.7	$ 18.7
Iran	.74%	.85%	332.7	485.4
Iraq	3.13%	1.48%	405.6	224.8
Nigeria	1.03%	.15%	9.9	29.7
Venezuela	.21%	.08%	56.0	24.9
Average	.21%	.54%		
Total $			$ 846.9	$ 783.5
"Bankers"				
Kuwait	2.24%	2.75%	$ 274.8	$ 330.5
Libya	1.03%	1.62%	117.6	165.7
Qatar	4.33%	6.39%	86.5	147.0
Saudi Arabia	2.47%	2.64%	870.0	917.0
UAE	3.89%	4.60%	291.9	403.7
Average	2.80%	5.00%		
Total $			$1640.8	$1963.9

Source: Calculated from OECD, DAC Annual Review, 1976, p. 101.

lending benefited the richer Third World developing nations—export platforms like Mexico, Colombia, Korea, and Taiwan—as well as the OPEC nations themselves. Still, the international banks did attempt to provide their services to credit-worthy, less developed nations; international lending to the least developed countries (GNP per capita under $200 per year) in 1975 was $1.7 billion. While this figure remains rather low, it is seventeen times greater than in 1971, two times greater than in 1973, and three times greater than in 1974 (OECD, 1976:70). By the end of 1976, the seventy-one NODCs had borrowed $110 billion from private banking sources (Cleveland and Brittain, 1977:734).

Even the most destitute countries have found some credit with private bankers; however, many countries, such as Zaire, which is now nearly $4 billion in debt, have found it extremely difficult to service these debts once they have been contracted. Only direct financial stabilization by the IMF's planners and a new $250 million loan from Citibank of New York saved Zaire from total default in 1976 (Beim, 1977:727). Among Africa's NODCs, by January 1977, Egypt had borrowed $7.3 billion, Tanzania $.96 billion, Zaire $1.9 billion, and Zambia $1.2 billion as long-term credits from the international banks (Cleveland and Brittain, 1977:734). To be sure, these private flows took up some of the slack in the NODCs' current-account deficits since concessional aid in 1974 only financed four-fifths of their needs (OECD, 1976:45). As a result, all of the NODCs, including some of the African MSAs, have been driven into more expensive private flows of short-term trade credits and long-term bank loans which, as in the case of Zaire in 1976, will undoubtedly bring them to the brink of default under the hard-servicing terms of private-bank credit. If nothing else, the international banks' new role in the NODCs reveals the profound change in international aid flows after the 1973 oil-price crisis as the banks' share of total international aid in 1974-75 rose to 18 percent compared to nearly nothing in 1971. In the short run, the NODCs' retreat to the private banks represents an added margin of financial security as they lessened their exchange deficits and reopened their economies to foreign imports, which fell in 1973-74 to below 1970 levels and surpassed 1970 figures only in 1975 (OECD, 1976:45). Nevertheless, this additional foreign debt only aggravates the NODCs' already overextended debt-servicing situation now "equivalent to some 15 per cent of their export earnings" (OECD, 1976:46).

The major implication of the oil crisis in developmental programming, then, has been the change in the source and structure of aid flows. From 1970-71 to 1974-75, intergovernmental aid assistance dropped among the OECD DAC nations while rising somewhat among the OPEC countries, especially the "banker" Arab states of the Gulf region. The DAC area (Europe and North America) supplied 90.5 percent of average net bilateral flows in 1970-72; only 2.4 percent originated in the OPEC countries. By 1974, however, the ratio changed significantly. The DAC region supplied only 86.6 percent of all such aid, while the OPEC states more than doubled their efforts by providing 7.8 percent of all development aid. Of course, a radical reconstruction of aid flows did not materialize, but this change at the margin had tremendous impact on the NODCs, given the unusual "geographic concentration" of OPEC's expanded aid disbursements. OPEC aid commitments rose from $1.5 billion in 1973 to $9 billion in 1975; however, "Arab countries obtained three-fifths of total OPEC ODA [official development assistance] commitments both in 1974 and 1975" (OECD, 1976:62).

Hence, as the margin of international aid flows shifted, many countries were caught out in the cold, but most tragically, the African MSAs suffered from the drift of these changes. As EEC's aid through the OECD DAC programs dropped, the Arab OPEC states failed to make up the deficit as their aid went to Arab or Islamic NODCs. Indeed, the OPEC ODA flows in 1975 were concentrated in 35 countries—the top 5 states received 70 percent of the total aid payments. In contrast, among the OECD's ODA to 160 countries, the top 5 got less than 33 percent of the total (OECD, 1976:63). The OECD region gave 55 percent of its bilateral aid to the least developed NODCs, but OPEC diverted only 45 percent of its bilateral aid to the least developed NODCs, mainly to two countries: India and Pakistan (OECD, 1976:62). Consequently, the African MSAs have been pinned in an economic vise; the old flow of OECD DAC credit is less and spread out over more countries, while the OPEC flows of new developmental aid are greater but concentrated on only a few Arab or Islamic nations. Losing around 2.5 percent of their GNP in 1974-76 to the OPEC nations through higher petroleum prices, the NODCs are running a (cumulative) $16 billion trade deficit vis-à-vis OPEC, compared to a $3 billion deficit four years earlier in 1973 (OECD, 1976:38).

Both the OECD and OPEC nations apparently are attempting to target the poorest MSAs for assistance through the IMF, the IBRD, and the IFAD; still, OECD remains most committed to its industrial-export platforms in the Third World and "the mainstream of OPEC financial flows was not directed towards those countries which were hit hardest by the oil price increase" (OECD, 1976:100). In theory, the international aid flows through the OECD DAC states, the OPEC countries and the private banking sector, along with the quickened economy in 1975-76, have revived most of the NODCs' economies. Yet, in practice, "the variation in the impact of the oil price increase and of the recession, in the context of the large differences in borrowing capacity and the skewed distribution of official financing, particularly from OPEC, has led to mismatches between the need for external finance and its supply" (OECD, 1976:39).

5
Arab-African Relations and International Summitry

The political inspiration that the OPEC cartel gave to other commodity-producing and exporting countries, particularly those in Africa, has become a critical dimension in Arab-African relations since 1973. Both the Arab OPEC states and the African NODCs have been major proponents of the creation of a "new international economic order" (NIEO) through international summitry, integrated commodity agreements (ICAs), and commodity cartelization schemes. Consequently, in order to investigate the relationship of the Arab-African link to the NIEO, this section documents the issues and outcomes involved in six of the more important post-1973 international economic summits. The most fascinating aspect of these relations is the remarkable success of the Arab OPEC states in assigning the guilt for the NODCs' post-1973 economic hardships to the First World area—the Western industrial nations and Japan. By acting as the "moral leaders" of the financially prostrate NODC-MSA world at these international economic summits, and by encouraging these poor countries to emulate the example of OPEC, the Arab OPEC states largely have avoided being blamed by most poor countries for the NODCs' financial crises.

Still, given the Arab OPEC states' increasingly evident "embourgeoisement," many African countries have begun to realize that their Arab "moral leaders" are not delivering expected political payoffs at economic summits and that the Arab commitment to NODC development is not much more creditable than that of many of the First World nations. Hence,

Arab-African relations are cooling significantly as these international economic summits progress. Whereas the Sixth Special Session of the United Nations General Assembly, in May 1974, found many of the African states eagerly supporting the Arab OPEC countries in a collective bid to forge the NIEO, the Conference on International Economic Cooperation (CIEC) dialogue concluded in June 1977 with the Africans accusing the Arab OPEC states of turning the North-South discussions into an OPEC-OECD "talking shop" (*African Development*, 1976:127).

In May 1974, at the conclusion of the Sixth Special Session of the United Nations General Assembly, the African NODCs joined in with the other "Group of 77" members in proclaiming the need for a NIEO. Convoked by Algerian President Houari Boumedienne in April 1974, the Sixth Special Session celebrated OPEC's successful consolidation of its control over petroleum production and pricing by challenging the international economic order constructed by the OECD nations and accusing it of "being in direct conflict with current developments in political and economic relations" (Erb and Kallab, 1975:186), that is, in conflict with the economic interests of the "Group of 77." Even as the oil-price increase devastated the economies of the poorest countries, many NODCs seemed to relish greatly the psychological damage done to the First World as it suffered under increased oil prices and the constant threat of an OPEC embargo (*Los Angeles Times*, 8/31/75).

The Arab OPEC countries easily forestalled a potential backlash over higher oil prices in the LDCs with a tripartite strategy: (1) by playing up the political and psychological impact of OPEC's oil prices on the OECD economies; (2) by encouraging the NODC commodity producers to "do an OPEC" on the First World; and (3) by promising—but not always delivering—developmental aid drawn from the new petrodollar accounts. Clearly, the Sixth Special Session provided the Arab OPEC countries with a rare opportunity; in the midst of an oil-price crisis, they successfully portrayed the high cost of industrial goods and "colonial trade" relations with the OECD nations as the cause of the Fourth World's miseries. What is more, the Arab OPEC states also encouraged the Fourth World not to fight the high cost of oil, but rather to use their own commodity trade as a lever of power over the exploitative First World.

The Lomé Convention, negotiated during 1974 and signed in February 1975, provided the African countries with their first opportunity to test the OPEC thesis on the commodity "trade weapon." For most observers, the Lomé agreements between the Common Market (EEC) and the forty-five ACP (Africa, Caribbean, and Pacific) countries mark the African states' first ICA embodying the exercise of producer power. Unlike the previous Yaoundé and Commonwealth accords, Lomé's agricultural commodity scheme incorporated provisions for consultative, codetermined, and participatory trading decisions between the EEC and the ACP countries. Instead of having prices dictated by tariff or import decisions in the EEC region, the ACP states collectively determine changes in price, supply, and price-support arrangements (Green, 1976:44-45). In order to stabilize the EEC's import schedules and to stabilize ACP states' commodity export earnings, the ACP countries' export income is rationalized through payments made by the Stabex common fund.

The Stabex fund makes up the difference between price floors and actual market prices, thereby routinizing the commodity exporters' earnings. Although the Lomé Convention and the Stabex scheme were not the direct result of OPEC-style organization, these structures share many of the same principles and provide added support to the Fourth World's desire to rationalize their export industries as a means of accruing greater national income (Green, 1976:51-53). And, perhaps most important, the ACP states' skill in negotiating the Lomé agreements gave them a sense of exercising OPEC-like power. For the African commodity-exporting states, the Lomé accord is a considerable improvement over previous trade relations with the EEC—its benefits for the EEC notwithstanding—and the African NODCs have seen Lomé as "a sign of how strong the ACP countries have become relative to the EC [European Community] countries" (Galtung, 1976:41).

In concluding the Sixth Special Session, the attending nations proclaimed that

> The developing world has become a powerful factor that makes its influence felt in all fields of international activity. These irreversible changes in the relationship of forces in the world necessitate the active, full and equal participation of the developing countries in the formulation and application of all decisions that concern the international community (Erb and Kallab, 1975:186).

Still, in announcing these goals, the OPEC countries, especially Algeria and Venezuela, assumed, and were expected by the NODCs to assume, an entrepreneurial role in pressing these collective ideals into practical policy. To a very real extent, the NIEO ultimately was grounded in the OPEC paradigm of economic action—producers' cartels were to be used to coerce the First World into providing aid to accelerate the NODCs' economic development. As Somalia's delegate observed, "The action of the OPEC countries was a breakthrough in the efforts of the third world to correct the massive dominance of the industrialized countries in the world market for raw materials. It set the stage for the creation of a new economic order through cooperation between the developed and the developing countries on the basis of equality" (Renninger, 1976:37). The Seventh Special Session, however, came in December 1975, eighteen months after the heady days of May 1974 which had so brightly presaged collective action and organization among the NODCs. With the exception of the Lomé accords, the LDCs had achieved little progress in effecting "active, full and equal participation" with the First World nations.

We submit that the lack of progress was largely attributable to the new Third World of the OPEC states. Perhaps the most telling evidence, however, of OPEC's unwillingness to solidly back the Fourth World's efforts to form effective producer cartels came in Dakar in February 1975. There, at the First International Conference on Raw Materials, the OPEC states adamantly refused to fund common-fund schemes to stabilize commodity prices and to build buffer stocks for creating higher commodity prices. In other words, the OPEC states, on the one hand, had urged the LDCs to form their own OPECs; but, on the other hand, OPEC refused to supply the financial backing that would make these new OPECs a practical alternative. Moreover, OECD and OPEC aid to the NODCs was very slow in coming; the continuing recession in the OECD area made new trade agreements difficult to conclude; the OECD nations sought to weaken the OPEC states' new power by co-opting them into important financial and economic institutions; and the whole world had another year and a half of higher oil bills to pay to the OPEC countries. As the Seventh Special Session opened, the NODCs, "led by such militants as Algeria, Libya, and Iran, felt that the rich nations of the developed world could be forced into making concessions" (*African Development*, 1976:124). The aggressive tactics of the Sixth Session, however, failed to work on a more united OECD region, and "the attempt to win concessions by confrontation, by threatening a trades union of the Third World or Arab-financed producer cartels simply meant that no progress was made on the substantive issues in 1974" (*African Development*, 1976:124).

Consequently, the Arab OPEC states found much of their earlier support dissipating as the NODC delegates to the Seventh Special Session voiced their views about how to build a NIEO with OPEC's immense wealth. The NODCs continued to vote with the Arab OPEC states to maintain political solidarity, but many Africans began openly and pointedly to make complaints about the Arabs' intentions and actions. Speaking for the African NODCs on their dissatisfaction with OPEC's aid, Sierra Leone's foreign minister noted, "It is our view that the oil exporting countries must spearhead the third development decade" (Renninger, 1976:45). Voicing the same disenchantment, only more strongly, Zaire's foreign minister accused the OPEC nations of "strangling" the African NODCs' economies (Renninger, 1976:45). In sum, while giving apparent support to the Arab OPEC states' moves in favor of the NIEO, the Seventh Special Session saw many African leaders coming to agree with the American position on the OPEC price increase; that is, that "the 'enormous, arbitrary' increases in petroleum prices had 'shattered the economic planning and progress of many countries' " (Renninger, 1976:47).

Much of this disenchantment with the OPEC states was probably inevitable; ultimately, it had the beneficial effect of changing the NODCs' mood from one of confrontation to one of cooperative dialogue. The Session reaffirmed the call for a more equitable distribution of the world's production and passed a number of resolutions outlining means for redistributing, wealth, technology, and markets. The assembled nations agreed to liberalize trade relations in favor of the NODCs, to study commodity price-stabilization structures, to raise official foreign aid payments, to transfer more technology to the NODCs, to open decision-making procedures in the IMF, and to encourage more processing of commodities in the producing countries (Renninger, 1976:38). Undoubtedly, these resolutions represented a respectable achievement for the "Group of 77" in their dealings with the First World nations. Yet, at the same time, very few of these measures promised much immediate improvement for the African NODCs. For them, the most important outcomes of the Seventh Special Session came in the promises of commodity price stabilization, expanded processing of agricultural goods at the point of origin, liberalized trade, and increased aid agreements. In exchange, the African NODCs backed the OPEC states' call for more technology transfers, increased participation in institutions like the IMF, and more industrial investment in the non-industrialized world.

Plainly, UNCTAD IV, as it opened in Nairobi, Kenya, during May 1976, met in a very different world than that of UNCTAD III, held in Santiago, Chile, during April-May 1972. Nonetheless, even though separated by the oil crisis, OPEC, "stagflation," and the UN's Sixth and Seventh Special Sessions, UNCTAD IV continued the businesslike approach of UNCTAD III as the delegates concentrated their efforts on its main goal: structuring a system of ICAs whose outlines had been accepted nine months earlier at the Seventh Special Session.

Having realized the futility of confrontation tactics at the Sixth and Seventh Special Sessions, the policymakers of the

"Group of 77" settled down to engage in practical negotiations at UNCTAD IV. UNCTAD I, II, and III "achieved next to nothing: The Generalized Scheme of Preferences (GSP) which eliminated tariffs in the West on a wide selection of manufactured goods from the Third World; a Code of Conduct on shipping lines; and a Cocoa Agreement" (*African Development,* 1976:481). The GSP, unfortunately, failed to cover important NODC exports such as textiles; the Liner Code is almost totally ignored; and the Cocoa Agreement did not regularize cocoa exporters' earnings. Hence, the "Group of 77" hammered out four goals for UNCTAD IV at their pre-summit meeting in Manila during February 1976: (1) an $11 billion "buffer-stock" of commodities to stabilize prices; (2) indexation of raw materials against the prices of manufactured imports; (3) a compensation scheme along Lomé's Stabex guidelines for "loss of earnings" in commodity trade; and (4) lower tariffs on Third World manufactures in the First World market (*African Development,* 1976:481). The McIntyre Commonwealth Committee also called for the NODCs to concentrate on three points: the refinancing and rescheduling of debts, commodity stabilization, and greater industrial cooperation in processing commodities in the country of origin.

Somewhat chastened by their earlier failures to create an "instant" NIEO, the OPEC countries still led the "Group of 77" at UNCTAD IV; however, by this time, the Arab OPEC states had agreed that market management by producer-consumer negotiation was the best path toward effecting an NIEO. OPEC's own efficiency provided the basis for African commodity-producer power, but by now the Arab states realized that producer cartels on strict OPEC lines were not a practicable approach for the African NODCs. The African countries, once again, pinned their hopes on the clout wielded by the Arabs' oil weapon, but the outcome of UNCTAD IV gave them little immediate satisfaction. The OECD nations initially appeared positive about the common fund scheme, but reacted quite coolly to the Manila program because of the indexation proposal and the buffer stock funding arrangement. The debt issue was tabled pending additional technical advice, while the technology transfer accord asked for by the McIntyre Committee invited equivocation by the delegates over its voluntary or involuntary nature. Essentially, the UNCTAD IV discussions ended more in agreements to agree, pending further discussion, on a commodity stabilization arrangement and greater technical transfer—but no solid conclusions were reached. As UNCTAD IV concluded with more decisions postponed, many African states questioned the vision and efficacy of the "radical" OPEC countries' "moral leadership," and began listening to alternative proposals made by the OECD and the more moderate OPEC states.

In the face of obvious African discontent growing since the Seventh Special Session, the Arab states, led by the Arab OPEC countries, met in Cairo during March 1977 in a determined effort to shore up their authority and legitimacy among the African states. Dissatisfied with the Arabs' backing for their development needs, for the political struggle in southern Africa, and for their worsening financial difficulties, the African states clearly felt betrayed after supporting the Palestinians, celebrating OPEC's successes, and believing in the Arabs' promises of financial assistance.

That dissatisfaction was apparently first voiced officially, but privately, at the February 1975 meeting of the OAU Council of Ministers in Addis Ababa, at which it was decided that a special summit between African and Arab leaders should be arranged "to review further close relations between them." According to Colin Legum, "This decision was felt necessary because of the continuing frustrations of the attempts to reach agreements about institutional relations between the OAU and the Arab League required to coordinate their economic programmes and political policies. A majority of OAU members wanted the Arab oil compensatory aid to be channelled through the African Development Bank instead of the Arab League" (1976:A80). Moreover, leaks from the Ugandan, Tanzanian, and Cameroonian delegations revealed that not only was there unhappiness about the quality and quantity of Arab aid, but there was considerable feeling that donors and recipients should operate as equal partners. Assane Seck, Senegal's foreign minister, reportedly put the proposition in succinct, if blunt, terms: "The idea of being a beggar of the Arabs is not acceptable to Africans." Under the arrangements then in operation—the bulk of the funds disbursed through the Arab League—almost all the African states feared a cooperation agreement that would link Africa to the political problems of the Arab world (Legum, 1976:A81). A compromise agreement was finally drawn up and submitted to the July 1976 Kampala Summit of the OAU but, given the troubled atmosphere of that meeting, was not discussed. The 1977 Cairo Summit did finally discuss and pass it, but not before its intent was further clouded by events at the summit itself.

In any case, recognizing that good relations with Africa are "essential to their political and economic power" (MEED, 3/18/77:7), the Arabs convened the Afro-Arab Summit to put African and Arab economic and political cooperation on an institutional basis, as well as to dispel African insecurities about being slighted. In calling the meeting to order, Egyptian President Sadat enjoined the Arab and African states to cooperate more fully in order to be more credible as a bloc in dealing with the OECD nations. To defuse the Africans' dissatisfactions about the Arabs' restrained petrodollar disbursements, Sadat suggested "that no single bloc or nation should draw up lists of profits or losses"; rather, all Arab and African countries "should think of profits for all the 60 nations combined" (*Arab Economist*, 1977:22).

The African nations, however, remained unconvinced. Togo's foreign minister set the tempo for the African states by calling for substantial foreign aid without strings attached, and not as a reward for a pro-Arab political stand (*Arab Economist*, 1977:22). Although Arab aid to Africa up to 1977 had rested largely on political premises, the Arab states present in Cairo had agreed to a new nonpolitical formula. Tanzania's foreign minister proved even more aggressive by demanding $2.2 billion in economic aid for Africa over the next four years— four times the amount originally offered by the Arabs in the days preceding the Cairo Summit. However, in a dramatic move that underscored the newfound influence of the moderate "banker" Arab states, Saudi Arabia pledged $1 billion to African economic assistance. In turn, Kuwait, Qatar, and the

UAE pledged an additional $453 million to African aid programs (MEED, 3/18/77:7). In addition to these major financial promises, the Arabs also signed four accords with the African countries, including agreements on greater political cooperation, joint trade, preferential trade considerations, and institutionalized meetings every three years to maintain Afro-Arab solidarity (*Arab Economist,* 1977:23).

While appearing conciliatory toward the African countries, the Arabs again did not fully meet African expectations. Once more, the Africans received only pledges of aid, not immediate disbursements. The Arab pledges to development banks favored the Arab-dominated, Khartoum-based BADEA and not the African-controlled, Abidjan-based African Development Bank (ADB). The Saudis' participation in BADEA was raised by $120 million to $240 million; however, their participation in ADB was raised $10 million to $20 million. Clearly, Saudi Arabia "doubled" its participation in both banks, but the Arabs' BADEA was much favored over the Africans' ADB by twelve to one (MEED, 3/11/77:19). Of the $1.45 billion promised to the Africans, only $11 million was marked for African liberation movements in southern Africa (*Arab Economist,* 1977:23). Furthermore, the Arabs made no concessions on oil pricing, long-range aid commitments, or greater support for southern African liberation groups. Having demanded increased Arab deposits in ADB, the Africans simply received more bilateral aid links to the Arab OPEC states, further deposits in the Arab-controlled BADEA, more aid commitments but no disbursements, and only a promise of two-thirds of the $2.2 billion requested. Once again, the African NODCs came out on the short end of the deal, but they could not complain too openly because they did, after all, get something. Still, the Arab OPEC states' strategy at Cairo clearly continues their policy of making minimal deployments of aid and always on their own terms. Within OPEC, the moderate states retained their diplomatic preeminence by providing the Africans with funds; yet, their continuation of a "false promises" policy may also tarnish their image among the African countries. Finally, Colin Legum makes a useful comparison; the $1.45 billion pledged the Africans stands in contrast to Arab aid given non-African Muslim countries. In 1976 Saudi Arabia loaned Pakistan *alone* $1.7 billion to buy arms from the United States (1977:A105).

The Conference on International Economic Cooperation (CIEC) talks, begun in early 1977, grew out of European (especially French) desires to arbitrate "North-South" economic conflict through producing-consuming country dialogues. The Europeans' answer to the United States' strategy of forming the International Energy Agency, pushing alternative energy development, and working to split OPEC, the CIEC talks opened on the premise that the "Southern" countries have the right and the power to set and control their commodity prices. The main emphasis of the CIEC discussions was on the questions of energy and the OPEC cartel; however, both the OECD and OPEC nations insisted upon Fourth World representation in order to advance their own bloc's interests before the NODCs. The NODCs, on the other hand, hoped that the CIEC would become a more efficient alternative to the deadlocked UNCTAD and UN General Assembly discussions.

At the CIEC, the OECD nations consistently maneuvered to make an energy forum out of the conference by stressing the need to negotiate oil prices and supply and production priorities. The American plan to create an international energy institute to discuss energy needs and dispense technical aid on energy matters met with continual rebuff. The "Group of 19," representing the "Group of 77," refused to deal exclusively with energy issues at the CIEC. Instead, these states called for continuing discussions of energy problems at all levels of existing international organizations. Likewise, the "Group of 19" sought the indexation of oil prices and guarantees for maintaining the purchasing power of petrodollars in the OECD's industrial and financial markets. Simultaneously, the OPEC countries continued to reject the OECD's demands for joint consultation on energy questions.

It is plain that at the CIEC talks, the OECD, the OPEC, and the NODC states simply continued their intricate dance around the tough questions raised by the oil-price increase. The First

World nations evaded making concessions on the NIEO as they worked to break up OPEC and to discredit it before the NODCs by focusing on the oil problem. Similarly, OPEC attempted to maintain its position as the Fourth World's economic advocate and moral leader, while, at the same time, striving to force concessions out of the First World on price indexation and investment guarantees—which would only serve the OPEC countries' interests. The NODCs, by the same token, continued their offensive for the NIEO against the OECD, while lobbying with OPEC "to use its oil to force concessions from the industrialized countries" (MEED, 6/24/77:9). The CIEC talks, then, accurately reflected the political posturing of the world's new developmental tiers. The OPEC states—as newly "rich" countries with strong political ties to the "poor" countries— struggle to maintain their alliance with the LDC–Fourth World even though their interests are no longer quite the same. In testing its oil power against the OECD, OPEC's leaders realize their interests lie more with the First World than the new LDC–Fourth; yet, they continue their Fourth World ties to gain more influence in their dealings with the OECD. The OECD strives to split the OPEC-NODC alliance to maintain its own dominance and to obtain energy concessions. And, finally, the NODCs, suffering from higher oil prices and world recession, hitch their political hopes to the use of the OPEC states' power to win more aid from both OPEC and the OECD. Ultimately, these cleavages serve only to add to the power and prestige of the Arab OPEC states, not to help the most disadvantaged of their clients.

Consequently, the NODCs are becoming increasingly suspicious of the OPEC leadership's motives. The African countries have realized that the Arabs have now been ensnared by their embourgeoisement: Saudi Arabia worries mainly about its Western investments, Iran frets about the health of the OECD's financial structures, and Algeria now convenes meetings of the OECD and OPEC ministers, not NODC congresses. Indeed, despite their faith in the oil weapon, the NODCs suspect and distrust OPEC's desire for oil-price indexation and investment protection. They recognize that these measures would harm the Fourth World inasmuch as it is unable to cope with spiraling oil prices and has little income from foreign investments to protect. As the CIEC talks progressed, the African NODCs "showed that they felt that OPEC was ready to sell them down the river to the industrialized countries so that the CIEC could once again become the energy talking shop it had originally been intended to be" (*African Development,* 1976:129). The NODCs' distrust grew as the OPEC countries refused to adopt any solid policy-negotiating guidelines in the CIEC commissions and as the OPEC states took over most of the conference's four commissions' co-chairmanships: Saudi Arabia co-chaired the Energy Commission, Iran took the Finance Commission, and Algeria assumed co-chairmanship of the Economic Development Commission. Only the Raw Materials Commission went to a NODC, that is, Peru. As one observer asked, "what positions of responsibility were held by representatives of the hundreds of millions of people from Africa and Asia at the conference? None" (*African Development,* 1976:129).

At the final CIEC sessions, the OECD states, under American leadership, stuck to their strategy of dividing the "Group of 19" by blaming the world's economic doldrums on high oil prices. The OPEC states, on the other hand, claimed that "the cruelest blow to the developing countries has come not from oil prices but from higher costs of imported food, industrial manufactures, western services and capital goods" (*African Development,* 1976:127). The "Group of 19" largely resisted the OECD's pressures and stood behind the oil lever to wring concessions out of the OECD, especially its "hard-liners": the United States, the United Kingdom, Japan, and West Germany. The OPEC states backed a common fund for commodities, the end of OECD trade protection, and improving international financial institutions' decision-making processes to include nonindustrialized countries. Yet, as the talks broke off in June 1977, the OECD nations and the "Group of 77" slipped further into conflicts over the common fund for commodities, which prevented the resumption of discussion through mid-1978. Because of the deadlock over the funding of the common fund, informal talks were conducted at several international and regional summits as well as under the auspices of the Brandt Commission. However, formal talks remained impossible because of the intransigence of both sides (MEED, 5/19/78:15).

To be sure, certain advances were made at the CIEC talks. The United States, the United Kingdom, Japan, West Germany, Canada, and Australia joined with the seventeen other OECD nations who had acted at UNCTAD IV in favor of an integrated commodity-agreement program combined with a common-stocks buffer fund (adopted in principle at the London Summit in early 1977). The OECD also affirmed its pledge to raise its aid payments to .7 percent of GNP for each nation by 1980, or double the current .3 percent average (MEED, 6/13/77:9). A $1 billion special aid program—in combination with a promise from Canada, Switzerland, and Sweden to end the debt service on their loans to the least developed NODCs—also was constructed in exchange for the "Group of 19's" willingness to back down from a demand for relief of the NODCs' $180 billion debt. An energy cooperation program was accepted in principle, but was not defined; and discussions on stabilizing export earnings were agreed to, but not detailed.

To an important degree, then, the bases of Arab-African relations at international summits have changed significantly. No longer allied in common cause against Western colonialism, the Arab and African states maintain an uneasy union in the common search for a NIEO. While the OPEC nations are not completely loved, "their success sent a thrill of pride through the developing countries—even those, ironically, who were worst hit by the oil price rises" (*African Development*, 1976:482). Spurred on by images of OPEC-like success, the NODCs have labored extensively to act in united fronts—the ACP bloc, the "Group of 77," the "Group of 19," UNCTAD— to press their program for redistributing the world's wealth. Initially, the OPEC nations provided much of the inspiration and resources for these kinds of sessions; the "agent provocateur" rolé played by Algeria, Iraq, and Iran reaffirmed their self-image as "revolutionary" states and cultivated their legitimacy as the NODCs' guardians. After the CIEC, however, many NODCs in Asia and Africa are beginning to look for new "moral leadership" in the moderate Arab OPEC states, in Nigeria, or perhaps Venezuela. Clearly, the NODCs no longer trust most of the OPEC states' motives and actions with regard to building the NIEO for the benefit of the Fourth World.

6

The Arab Developmental World

In the 1960s, both academics and policymakers divided the world of nations into three distinct blocs of nation-states whose ranking in each bloc depended upon their respective national economic, political, and social power (Horowitz, 1965). A decade later, however, the events of the intervening years greatly weakened the accuracy of the "Three Worlds" scheme. The First World of Europe, Japan, and North America gradually was coming to pragmatic terms with the Second World of the Soviet Union and the other states that modernized through "socialist revolution." However, the greatest transformation occurred within the Third World of less developed and so-called nonaligned states of Africa, Asia, and Latin America.

Historically, the Third World's distinguishing features have been political domination by and economic dependence upon the more powerful First and, in some cases, Second Worlds. By the 1970s, however, certain Third World nations were making some considerable economic and political advances. A small group of "export platforms" (Barnet and Mueller, 1974:132, 194, 196)—states with high levels of foreign corporate investment which tied them into international trade networks—such as Mexico, Brazil, Korea, Taiwan, and Hong Kong, plus the oil-exporting countries, slowly were increasing their GNPs and their political visibility. Still, the Third World states remained "dual" economies and societies that blended modern corporate production with traditional peasant agriculture. Consequently, for the most part, the Third World states were realizing political independence, but not political autonomy; achieved economic growth, but not economic development; and effected social change, but not social progress.

The past seven years radically transformed this international hierarchy of states. A *new* Third World, a different developmental world, has emerged from the *old* dominated and dependent Third World. By its emergence, this upwardly mobile Third World is reconstituting the symmetries of global interdependence, thereby establishing new configurations in the international division of power and status. The states of the Organization of Petroleum Exporting Countries (OPEC)— Saudi Arabia, Iran, Iraq, Kuwait, Abu Dhabi, Qatar, Algeria, and Libya, as well as Gabon, Nigeria, Ecuador, Venezuela, and Indonesia—form the core of the new developmental world. With the formation of this new bloc, the vast majority of the less developed nations in Africa, Asia, and Latin America have undergone downward mobility to become the clients and constituents of the new Third World and to become a new Fourth World, in effect the residual category of the transformation. Like the relatively self-sufficient First World, this new Fourth World awoke in 1973 to the presence of a new set of dependency relations—those involving both modern and modernizing economies' oil-supply needs now largely under the price control of the OPEC states. Here, we examine how the new Third World has turned its command over most of the planet's petroleum resources—despite all of its political problems—into the economic, political, and social foundations of a new developmental bloc. Special attention will be paid to the Arab OPEC states, and to the parallels of their development with those of the First and Second Worlds, in order to better comprehend the motives behind their relations with the First and Fourth Worlds.

October 1973 marks the birthdate of the Arab developmental world. Still, in discussing the origins and operations of what amounts to an emerging developmental model, a very important fact must be kept constantly in mind, namely, that the emergence and maintenance of this developmental path *necessarily* depended on the existence of the developed First

World. In a very real sense, the Arab developmental world was conceived by the industrial states of Western Europe, Japan, and North America after World War II as their industrial economies increasingly shifted from coal to oil to satisfy their energy needs. Moreover, this developmental path depended heavily upon the activity of the large transnational oil corporations which so eagerly engineered the First World's increasing dependence upon the petroleum they produced and marketed. So effective were the corporations that by 1973 Europe relied on oil to generate 60 percent of its energy, of which 98.7 percent was imported oil with some 69 percent of that supply coming from the Arab states (Remba, 1976:30-31). Japan depended on oil for 76 percent of its energy, nearly 100 percent of which was imported; 72 percent of its needs were filled by Middle East suppliers (Remba, 1976:30-31). The United States used oil for 47 percent of its energy needs, of which 35 percent was imported with nearly 10 percent of these imports coming from the Middle East (Remba, 1976:30-31). The solid structure of these international oil markets, then, provided the ultimate basis for the Arabs' developmental strategy.

Originally organized in Baghdad during September 1960, OPEC was designed as a mechanism for protecting its members' mutual interests against the collective actions of the transnational oil corporations (TNCs) which have operated as a price and production "cartel" in the world market since the 1920s. Initially, OPEC was ineffectual against the allied operations of the "seven sisters" of transnational oil (Blair, 1976), but it slowly gathered strength during the 1960s under the political guidance of Iran, Venezuela, Iraq, Kuwait, and Saudi Arabia. The political potential of OPEC became manifest in 1971 in Tehran and Tripoli as the OPEC nations successfully forced a limited price increase upon the hitherto united and resistant oil companies. Further clout was created and exercised in Riyadh during 1973 as the OPEC nations sought gradual full "participation" in the ownership and management of the TNCs' joint venture subsidiaries such as ARAMCO.

Still, it required the October war and the ensuing OPEC oil

embargo to fix the necessary conditions for the postnatal survival of this new developmental world. The technical prerequisites preceded the birth of the new world by several months (Blair, 1976:268-81), but the events of October 1973 cast the suitable political climate for its final appearance. With Arab armies "victorious" for the first time against Israel, with the transnational oil companies acceding to its directives, and with its often factious and diverse membership acting as one, OPEC unilaterally declared a 70 percent increase in the price of the globe's main energy source—OPEC, but especially Arab, petroleum.

The initial price hike from $3.00 to $5.11 a barrel was augmented on January 1, 1974, with an additional increase bringing the posted price per barrel to $11.65 (Blair, 1976:262). As Blair notes, the implications for the transfer of wealth implied by the new prices were traced in 1974 by the *Petroleum Economist*: "the producing countries stand to increase their revenues to well over $100 billion in 1974 if production goes ahead as planned before the cutbacks, compared with the $30 billion they would have received on the basis of the posted price level on 1st October, 1973, and $51 billion after the 16th of October increase" (Blair, 1976:272). Forecasts by the World Bank in July 1974 projected that "the OPEC countries would accumulate an exchange surplus of $643 billion by 1980 and of $1.2 trillion by 1985" (Blair, 1976:273). In juxtaposition to OPEC's net foreign assets of $20 billion in 1973 and of $5 billion in 1970, it becomes clear that the oil-producing states, especially the Arab countries, stood to control an unprecedented flow of financial resources for their respective developmental programs.

Plainly, these early estimates of the OPEC states' financial windfall have proved exaggerated. Even with further price increases in 1975 and 1976, the OPEC economies are accumulating less financial power than was originally expected. Most of the funds they have gathered are being prudently recycled for industrial goods or are reinvested carefully in world commercial and financial centers; current estimates peg the total 1980 petrodollar surplus at only $200 to $250 billion (Tucker, 1977:23). Nonetheless, the important fact remains, namely, that OPEC's mode of earnings is a new form of capital accumulation which, in turn, animates the development of an entirely new bloc of modernizing states. However, the Arab countries' developmental success can be understood only by recognizing that they *are* and *were* Fourth World nations prior to or apart from their involvement with their primary developmental agents—the transnational oil corporations. That is, their most characteristic quality is that of a dual economy. Ouside of the petroleum sector, in many respects, the Arab OPEC states continue to have traditional economies and societies as poor as any in the Fourth World.

Still, because of their oil reserves, the Arab nations, in a very real way, did *not* need to internally generate the requisite elements of development: a skilled labor force, technical expertise, native capital reserves, and a popularized developmental ideology. All of these elements existed in, and could be obtained from, Europe, Japan, North America, or even the Communist states. Hence, a historical compromise for national development was struck between the more advanced and the more backward nations through the mediation of the TNCs. The newly independent oil-producing Arab states, prior to the TNCs' penetration, were so backward that even their state structures could not serve as the foundation of development. Therefore, their ruling elites turned to the oil-consuming nations' petroleum corporations as a structural substitute to start their very much delayed industrialization. The Arab political leaders granted the corporations generous territorial and economic concessions, and, in turn, the TNCs provided the initial capital, the skilled labor, the technical expertise, and the outlines of a developmental ideology which detonated the explosive developmental process of the Arab states.

The TNC is excellently adapted to act as the structural mediation of national development. The eight "major" oil companies and their former regional subsidiaries, which have now been "indigenized" as ARAMCO, INOC, NIOC, KNOC, and ADNOC, are creatures of international corporate, not nation-state, activity and loyalty. As such, they owed their existence and success to operating in the oil-producing

countries for their parent TNC combines, and *not* for the
TNCs' ultimate customers, the oil-consuming nations. The
TNCs were, and to a certain extent still are, the Arab states'
primary capital generators and accumulators. Through
corporate internal savings and later through international
commercial banks, the TNCs imported pump-priming capital
into the Arab economies. By opening their resources to foreign
development, the TNCs also imported skilled labor, technical
experts, and capital goods which were necessary for refining,
transporting, managing, and marketing these resources. Still,
as the TNCs' administration and production needs grew, these
corporate structures necessarily drew upon native labor and
talent. Whereas the Arab states, even the military-ruled states,
had failed to mobilize their capital and labor resources, the
TNCs easily mobilized and absorbed a great many locally born
workers, training them to control and manage modern
corporate and industrial structures. Slowly, the TNC trade and
managerial schools, the on-the-job training in the oilfields,
and the massive deployment of modern capital goods allowed
many Fourth World nomads, peasants, and villagers to
transform themselves into drillers, pipeline engineers, industrial managers, and petroleum economists of the new Third
World. In so doing, these newly trained workers gradually
followed the cues of TNC administrative practices and
managerial theories to learn a new developmental ideology. As
concrete examples of modern management, rational administration, corporate power, large-scale organization, technological entrepreneurialism, and transnational oligopoly, the
TNCs tacitly projected the essentials of a growth-minded and
industrially oriented developmental ideology into the ranks of
the Arab modernizing elites. In their years of expansion in the
Arab states, the TNCs baited the Arabs' desire for modernity by
exposing many to the privileges of their own welfare systems
within the oil company communities in Saudi Arabia, Iran,
and around the Gulf (MEED, *Special Report*, 1976:20). At the
same time, the TNCs taught the OPEC states a great many
lessons in how to collectively program their goals just as the
corporations collectively administered the world's energy
resources to their own corporate advantage and to the
disadvantage of the oil-consuming First World.

Yet, through nationalization or participation, the Arab states are transcending their historical substitute to enter a more sophisticated phase of development, namely, that of state-organized and state-directed industrial development. The TNC presence over the past four decades gathered the finance capital, trained the skilled labor force, transferred the technical know-how, installed the capital goods, and stimulated the developmental ideology necessary for national Arab elites to exert their autonomous political control. The Arabs, and the other oil producers, have built OPEC as their "safety net" to coordinate collective transnational corporate action. As the former TNC oil ventures were increasingly subject to nationalization in the 1970s to guarantee Arab control over oil production and oil exporting, OPEC gained immense importance as the oil-producing nations' device for rationalizing their policies regarding the distribution and supply of oil. The major TNCs performed this supply prorationing and market-sharing function prior to OPEC's rise. To maintain the collective control engineered by the TNCs, OPEC is crucial to the transnational solidarity of the newly autonomous oil-producing states in pricing, supply, and production policies. As Zuhayr Mikdashi comments:

> In the nineteen-seventies, however, once full control over the oil industries had been achieved, the OPEC conference, the secretariat, and the common commission became as concerned about the "business" of oil as they already had been with its "politics." The business of oil *inter alia* called for expert skills in devising optimal pricing, production, and financial policies. For these, the OPEC governments came to rely on the technical staff of their newly formed national petroleum companies and of their central banks. OPEC delegations began to be composed of national corporation executives and bankers rather than politicians and bureaucrats of earlier years (1975:205-67).

The fact that the Arab states had enough personnel and resources to staff both their own national petroleum companies as well as contribute to OPEC's operations suggests that the Arab states were very capable of mastering their own developmental programs. Trained in the tradition of the TNC's operations, OPEC personnel and planning easily became the structural substitute of the historically constructed TNC oligopoly. To be sure, the TNCs still play an important role in exploring for and marketing oil worldwide, but the Arab states now effectively administer the production and exporting links in their national petroleum industries which, in turn, anchor their respective plans for further heavy industrialization. Furthermore, their transnational control apparatus, OPEC, frequently has "proved its competence in both 'battling' and 'cooperating' with the transnationals" (Mikdashi, 1975:206). Consequently, to best insure economy in the deployment of their scarce resources, the Arab OPEC states are infatuated with "bigness," which is reflected in an emphasis on large-scale industrial plants and capital-intensive modes of operation. Partly the result of purchasing capital goods and advanced technology from the already industrialized countries, and partly the result of a backward state making the fullest use of its scarce resources, these trends also appear to characterize the Arab developmental model as the following points illustrate in greater detail. The developmental model outlined here, which describes structural elements in the Arab oil states' economies and societies, complements the detailed outline of the Saudi economy recently provided by Sharshar (1977). The limited but strict constraints imposed on business activity by the Shari'a, the holy law (Sharshar, 1977:47-48), have not in any way hindered the development of an etatist mercantilism, nor prevented the kind of basic borrowing from the West and the TNCs that we describe. In fact, the Saudi government, in its first five-year plan, emphasizes the point:

> The Kingdom's commitment to the free enterprise economy is founded basically on Islamic guidelines and tradition. The Kingdom has concluded that the economy could not exploit fully the opportunities open to it except through the full utilization of private initiative, and by inducing private enterprises of all sizes and forms to perform the activities which it could perform more efficiently than the government (cited by Sharshar, 1977:48).

Basically, these trends can be subdivided into two sets: (1) the economic traits relating to finance capital, entrepreneurialism, industrialization, and organization, and (2) the political features regarding internal social forces, time frames, social costs, and embourgeoisement.

Sustained capital accumulation is a most essential element of development. The Arab states are engaged in "oil-drum accumulation" as their increasing share of posted petroleum prices swells their national savings of finance capital. In 1957, the average price per barrel of Saudi crude was less than $2; it is now over $12. Saudi Arabia's annual revenues two decades ago were $300 million a year; 1977's revenues should surpass $40 billion (MEED, 3/11/77:11). Kuwait's oil earnings in 1977 should reach at least $20 billion (MEED, 3/11/77:7). To judge the extensiveness of "oil-drum accumulation," for Saudi Arabia alone in October 1976, its total foreign assets were $46,669 million (MEED, 1976:27). Although OPEC's total investable surplus as a percentage of revenue fell from 59.7 percent in 1974 to 28.4 percent in 1977, nearly $158,000 million is invested worldwide with about a third of that sum in the United States (MEED, 9/30/77:11). As Saudi Arabia's oil production has risen from 1 million barrels per day (mbd) in 1958 to 3.5 mbd in 1970 to 8.2 mbd in 1976, a readily increasing supply of finance capital has accumulated as well (MEED, *Special Report*, 1976:27). The existence and exigencies of the world energy market lets the Arabs accumulate vast supplies of capital with few domestic social costs. The Arab peasants do not feel the hardest bite, but "average consumers" abroad, both American commuters and African peasants, do. OPEC's political ability to "assure the protection of their common oil interests, especially prices and oil-export revenues" (Mikdashi, 1975:203), has terminated the Arab states' respective histories as Fourth World countries. As a bloc of nation-states, the Arab countries are no longer being "decapitalized" by the dominant metropole of more advanced industrial nations. Instead, the Arab developmental world has turned the tables on the First World as Arab industrialization forms from the capital extracted by higher oil prices and reinvested oil revenues in the First World economy.

Equally essential to accumulating and controlling finance, the Arab states have produced whole groups of "finance capitalists," or an entrepreneurial elite capable of shrewdly using Arab capital resources for commercial and industrial applications. Oil moneys no longer lie inactive in the treasure rooms of minor sheikhs, or in the bullion vaults of Western banks. The Arabs, beginning with the original lessons learned at the Middle East Supply Center during the Second World War, have trained hundreds of students at schools ranging from the London School of Economics to Harvard Business School to the American land-grant universities in order to aggressively invest their capital worldwide. The managerial classes educated to administer the oil pipelines and oilfields in the 1960s have been transformed, in part, during the 1970s into entrepreneurial elites. As one Gulf Arab banker asserted, "To me, money is like an army. We deploy chunks of our money in certain areas of secure investment. Profit is our prime target. But if we ever lose—and loss is a fact of present-day markets, just as profit is—we plan our investment in such a way that the loss affects profits percentage alone, while capital itself remains intact for another round" (*Arab Economist*, 1976:28). Riyadh and Bahrein are now world centers of financial activity. In these financial markets, the Arabs have retreated from unstable gold and real estate buys to investing in common stocks, establishing joint banking agencies, purchasing large interests in industrial combines, and edging into international shipping ventures.

These new reserves of finance capital are further developing and expanding Arab entrepreneurial elites and structures. In 1975, Saudi Arabia earned over $35 billion from its oil exports, but only spent about $6 billion on its own national expenditures—the remainder had to be reinvested (Sheehan, 1976:116). Having taken command of their own oil production, the Arab states are working to control "downstream" distribution and transportation of oil. At this time, the Arab OPEC states refine only 12.6 percent of their oil production and maintain only 3.6 percent of the world's refining capacity (MEED, 2/10/78:17). Thirty percent of world shipping is to and from the Arab states, 90 percent of that volume in oil. Yet, the Arab states control only 2 percent of the world's fleet and carry only 5 percent of the traffic to and from the Middle East (MEED, 1/20/78:14). Hence, the Arab countries are beginning to diversify by financing tanker lines, crude-carrier construction, and even some limited marketing ventures (Oppenheim, 1976). The Abu Dhabi Fund for Economic Development, the Saudi Monetary Agency, the Kuwait Investment Company, and the Kuwait Fund for Arab Economic Development are financial institutions involved in funding and managing both Arab and Fourth World economic development. The further industrialization of Arab countries now is being planned, financed, and administered by Arab financiers and entrepreneurs, not First World investing elites. Such new developments as the Arab Monetary Fund and a commonly organized financial market to better allocate all the Arab states' growing capital reserves are additional indications of the Arab states' entrepreneurs' control over their economic futures through their own devices (MEED, 12/31/76:9).

As they begin their industrialization, the Arab states have particular advantages in their ability to tap into the present stage of technological development. With mainly small populations that lack many industrial skills, the Arab states could not have industrialized in more labor-intensive modes of industrial development. Yet, now these countries can more easily engage in industrialization by turning their surplus oil revenues into a highly capital-intensive industrial base.

As the most recent case of delayed industrialization, the Arab states are displaying a clear preference for large-scale industrial undertakings, big industrial plants, and high capital intensiveness. Some variation exists, to be sure. Smaller countries like Kuwait and Saudi Arabia need high technology to compensate for their very small labor forces, while larger states such as Algeria, Iraq, and even Iran are striving to build large heavy-industrial sectors to employ their larger populations. The Arabs' desire for large-scale industrialization is reflected in Saudi Arabia's $142 billion Second Development Plan and its Joint Commission on Economic Cooperation with the United States. In this plan, for example, ARAMCO has undertaken a $16,000 million natural-gas liquefaction scheme for export and use at the Saudis' industrial centers of Jubail and Yenbo. This massive project will feed energy into a planned petrochemical, fertilizer, and steel-mill complex in addition to supplying power stations and allied industries.

Foreign contractors perform much of the construction, but Arab engineers and ARAMCO planners have set out the designs and specifications (MEED, *Special Report,* 1976:20). Additionally, the Saudis, in conjunction with the American Joint Commission, are plotting out the large-scale development of infrastructure and service industries: "The activities of the commission include planning the needs and supply of electrical equipment, vocational training (particularly in engineering, agricultural and water resources planning, statistical assistance and data processing), creating a national park, the developing of food marketing and many other aspects of commerce, expanding radio and television networks, and advising on an intercity expressway road system" (MEED, *Special Report,* 1976:31-32). Saudi Arabia's new international airport, costing three to four billion dollars and planned to be as large in area as the District of Columbia, also indicates the Arabs' fascination with "bigness" in their rapidly progressing industrialization (Sheehan, 1976:117).

For the Arabs, then, industrialization means *heavy* industrialization with a concomitant interest in large-scale plants, or indeed whole industrial cycles. Because of their capital resources, and unlike Fourth World countries, the Arab states and Iran[8] do not think in terms of a petroleum refinery, a steel mill, a copper mine, or a power station. Rather, they are planning for and developing now entire petrochemical industries, whole steel sectors, full-blown copper industries, and comprehensive power networks in order to make rapid and efficacious use of their obviously dwindling oil resources. Egypt, Bahrein, and Iraq have large aluminum-refining operations on line, and Dubai, Iraq, Libya, and Saudi Arabia are also taking advantage of their cheap energy to build aluminum-processing industries (MEED, 1/20/78:10). Iran has allocated many billions of dollars for a nuclear-based electricity network; it also has invested in mines and refineries to tap its estimated three billion tons of copper reserves, while

over three billion dollars is earmarked for Iranian petrochemical industries by 1980 (*New York Times*, 1/30/77:11).

There also is a strong emphasis placed on "turn-key"
operations and emplacements that can be fitted immediately
into the productive process. The joint inter-Arab commissions
established to coordinate regional industrial activity reflect the
need for "bigness" and large-scale production as well. The
Industrial Development Center for Arab states in Cairo is
promoting investment in special and alloy steel industries to
satisfy internal market demands up to 1990, the Arab Mining
Company is running several operations in Arab countries, the
OAPEC ministers have agreed to organize petroleum services
for the Arab market through the Arab Petroleum Services
Company, and the Arab League has set up the Arab League's
Arab Union for Food Industries in Cairo to encourage regional
production, distribution, and marketing of food products. The
message of all these programs is the same—the greatly delayed
Arab industrialization has prompted them to stress large-scale
big industry and high capital intensiveness in their industrialization to overcome the lack of expertise, labor, and entrepreneurial skills among the Arab populations.

A final economic-related trend among the Arab states is their
tendency to plan and organize their industrial and commercial
activities in terms of the TNC model of organization. The
formerly a-national joint ventures constructed by the international oil industry in the Arab states have been absorbed
wholly into the Arab state structure, giving these former TNCs
a national economic role. In doing so, however, these TNCs
have strongly influenced the Arab states' economic and
political activities. Many of the organizational forms, procedures, and practices of Arab economic development are
basically corporate-inspired. OPEC, OAPEC, and a bevy of
other international councils and regional directorates that
coordinate and mediate the Arab states' development attest to
the impact of this inspiration.

On the basis of the TNC example, the Arabs have established
the Arab Mining Conference to discuss joint mining ventures
(MEED, 3/11/77:12), the Arab Economic Unity Council to
collectively plan economic interactions until 1981 (MEED,

12/31/77:9), the Arab Industrial Conference to organize regional industry (MEED, 1/7/77:9), the Arab Free Zones to promote inter-Arab trade (MEED, 3/11/77:22), the Arab Investment Company to manage public investments (MEED, 12/3/76:9), the Arab Monetary Fund (MEED, 12/3/76:8), and the Gulf Common Market to ease inter-Arab trade flow (MEED, 12/3/76:8). All of these agencies strive to impart a transnational corporate effect to Arab economic life. Through these organizations' activities, the Arab states' technical personnel bring collective management, rational administration, and large-scale organization to bear on their common economic and social challenges, much like the TNCs traditionally operated in the Middle East. What is more, these structures further bind the Arabs' cultural unity with functional ties of industry, finance, technology, commerce, and planning, enabling these rather small separate states to behave more like a single united body.

These four commonly developing economic trends, in turn, are closely related to an emerging set of political features shared by the Arab OPEC states. The peculiar tendencies of Arab industrialization directly affect the Arabs' internal social forces, time frames, social costs, and embourgeoisement.

In spite of the fact that world economic conditions and individual national objectives enforce a degree of Arab unity, an important diversity among their internal social forces exists within the Arab developmental world. Basically, two distinct classes of states, with two different internal alignments of social forces, coexist within this bloc's ranks: the "banker" and the "industrializer" nations (Blair, 1976:280-82).

The "banker" states share these common qualities: small populations, small agricultural bases, no significant peasant class, little previously established industry or infrastructure, small recently formed middle-class groups, but immense reserves of petroleum. To date, these nations mainly have been ruled by conservative aristocratic governments with deep commitments to traditional Islamic culture. They have accumulated large capital and foreign-exchange holdings, and they have a limited capacity for absorbing extensive heavy industrial development. Among this group of states are

Kuwait, Saudi Arabia, the UAE, Qatar, and Libya (which, of course, is an exception to many of the generalizations advanced above). At this time and in the future, this tier of states can be counted upon to break into the commercial-bank phase of development because of their large financial holdings, their small populations and work forces, and their commitment to traditional Islamic life. Financial and commercial ventures, turning on a white-collar economy and based on services, provide the "banker" countries with their most effective path for modern economic success without many of the disruptions caused by full industrialization. Indeed, the fact that they have such large reserves of oil and money accounts in part for their continuing aristocratic rule. There is plenty of opportunity and privilege available to the modernized middle-class groups, and a plethora of benefits open to the entire population because of these states' large supplies of oil. Hence, there has been little pressure to date for deposing the traditional ruling oligarchies.

The "industrializer" states, on the other hand, have a distinctly different configuration of internal social forces. Algeria, Iraq, and Iran fit into this category as already partially developed economies with large populations and sizable agricultural bases. Because of outside pressure and influence, these states possessed some infrastructure and industrial emplacements prior to experiencing a jump in their oil revenues; and they have articulated investment policies rooted in these oil moneys that aim at attaining much greater and more diverse levels of industrialization. Yet, their reserves of oil (with the probable exception of Iraq) are far more limited than the "banker" states', and they can absorb all of their oil receipts plus additional capital, as Algeria's and Iran's heavy foreign borrowing reveal. The "social costs" of modernization in these states—calculated in terms of peasant dislocations, rural poverty, police repression, urban sprawl, and internal resistance—are far greater than in the "banker" states.

The "industrializer" states' middle, working, and technical classes are comparatively much larger than the "banker" states', but these urban classes are still outnumbered heavily by the rural populations. To be sure, this greater internal class differentiation is reflected in the "industrializers'" civil-military governing alliances which are far more secular and radically oriented than those in the "banker" states. Iran surely was a traditional aristocratic regime, but its "White Revolution" and its goal of great power status clearly distinguished it from Saudi Arabia's puritanical Wahabbi regime. Ultimately, all of these nations aim at complete and comprehensive industrialization within the next generation. And, to be sure, a much greater sense of urgency prevails upon the "industrializer" states because their grand industrial programs are predicated upon relatively meager existing reserves of petroleum.

Within both blocks of states, however, a similar alliance of class forces has guided the process of development. The Arab model of high capital-intensive development has not necessitated the complete displacement of old ruling elites. In the "industrializer" states where more radical civil-military alliances succeeded colonial or aristocratic rule, the new rulers maintained essentially the same relations with the TNC structures. The TNC presence over the years has trained and employed a new class of managers, economists, engineers, and entrepreneurs, which are allied with an equally small working class; the working class, in turn, due to the capital intensiveness and technical sophistication of the petroleum industry, behaves much like a privileged petty bourgeoisie—and modern international higher-management groups. Together this unlikely alliance formed beneath the rule exercised by either traditional aristocratic regimes or civil-military modernizers within the Arab states as these rulers slowly prepared to assert national control over the TNCs' productive structures.

Once nationalization or participation began, the corporately created middle and working classes allied themselves with their states' established ruling elites to operate the oil industries for native benefit. The traditional aristocratic regimes, such as Saudi Arabia, Kuwait, and Qatar, try to limit change to the area of economic development so as to preserve Islamic culture, whereas the military-based rulers, such as in Algeria and Iraq, aim at using their economic development as a means to attain full social and cultural modernization. Still, for both internal class alignments, a dual economy-society relationship has survived the nationalization of the TNCs since most of the Arab populations, with the exception of Kuwait, live without many of the benefits of development. As the native middle and working classes have taken over the TNCs' operations in the Arab states, a good deal of the "separate utopia" syndrome persists as these new classes enjoy company housing, schools, and benefits, while the larger society of migrants, peasants, and nomads have received fewer social benefits. This question is one the ruling internal social forces are increasingly having to deal with as their national development accelerates.

The national leaderships of states that have experienced a delayed industrialization impose the constraint of limited developmental time frames on their populations as they initiate development. Usually, the ruling developmental elites impose or set a time frame for industrialization because of the tremendous pressures rapid industrialization puts on the people's political loyalties and social unity. One generation's satisfactions are postponed to insure greater material well-being for the next. The Arab states sense an equal urgency in their industrialization, but for different reasons. Once oil is lifted from their territory, it is gone forever; oil that remains in the ground if and when the First World develops any of its wide range of energy alternatives will be wasted potential. Consequently, the Arabs are not striving to industrialize quickly because of the high social costs that will be involved to overcome backwardness, but because their future prosperity is dependent upon a presently wasting resource. If the oil runs out before the secondary and tertiary industrialization takes solid hold, the Arabs stand to fall back into the ranks of the Fourth World. As the Shah of Iran continually observed, "our oil is bound to finish some day—in 20 or 30 years" (*New York Times*, 1/30/77:11). Industrial diversification and integrated economic planning, then, are in the works to assure equal power and prosperity for future generations of OPEC state citizens.

Only Algeria and Iraq have any kind of balanced economy at this time; both, like Iran, have considerable agricultural potential and large populations which could support an autonomous industrial state. Therefore, Algeria is building metal and mineral sectors as well as machine-tool and machinery industries to prepare for its non-oil-based industrialization. In its currently formulated new five-year plan, Algeria also is investing heavily in human services and education in order to prepare its population for industrial life (MEED, 6/2/78:3). Iraq, on the other hand, is striving to rationalize its considerable agricultural resources. The smaller, less populous states, Kuwait, Saudi Arabia, Qatar, the UAE, and Libya, are directed toward building more moderate industrial bases tied to petroleum: petrochemicals, fertilizers, food processing, shipping, and oil production. Also, commercial and financial services are projected as integral components of their economies: banking, common stocks, communications, and transportation industries. Having more oil in reserve for the future and more money in the bank presently, these states also hope to industrialize rapidly, but their urgency is plainly less pressing because of their financial security.

By and large, and quite unlike preceding forms of industrialization, the Arabs' accumulation of finance capital and formation of a modern work force have imposed fewer social costs on their native population. The plethora of oil moneys in most of these states has seen the construction of a welfare state proceed apace with the creation of an industrial state. Again, this turn of political events has come about largely because of the existence of the First World and its immediate concern for providing welfare services. Because the Arabs are developing under this distinctly different horizon of welfare priorities, they have plowed a great deal of investment into hospitals, housing, health services, schools, and welfare payments. Schools and hospitals are willingly built by the Arab states and, "though sometimes they cannot function for lack of staff, equipment or even water, illiteracy among the young is being abolished and health care is much superior to a decade ago" (Sheehan, 1976:118). Many of the benefits, to be sure, are reserved for the Arab states' citizens and many migrant Arab and African laborers receive few if any benefits, but the main trends are toward providing material benefits immediately to the population as the states industrialize. Indeed, such purchases reverberate the economic trends discussed above as social welfare services are planned for and provided on a large-scale capital-intensive basis to illustrate the Arabs' desire to overcome their delayed industrialization. Not only must they have the best industrial goods and technology available, they also must have the most up-to-date medical, educational, and health services.

The developmental substitutes deployed by the Arabs enabled them to diminish greatly their social costs in industrialization. Historically, the process of development has required a harsh redistribution from consumption to capitalization, the exploitation of rural agricultural production to fuel urban industrial expansion, and the delay of social gratifications for entire generations of citizens. In the Arab developmental world, however, the TNCs' importation of capital, labor, expertise, and developmental ideology placed an easy down payment on the Arabs' developmental advance. The continuing interest accruing from the TNCs' principal investments in infrastructure, capital goods, and labor training programs so far have obviated the Arab states' need to borrow against their domestic population's future social consumption.

At first, the TNCs both owned and controlled their capital, but, once it was fixed into place, the national elites began to assert national control and ownership to derive native benefits. Private wealth and public consumption in the Arab societies were not tyrannically expropriated by the ruling Arab elites; rather, TNC productive forces were increasingly turned to public advantage through added royalty assessments, the imposition of higher taxes, demands for limited participation, and, finally, by effecting full nationalization. Foreign capital, labor, and expertise were easily available, readily importable, and quite controllable once the Arab states worked for their collective benefit in unison. Saudi Arabia, for example, has over 1.5 million foreign laborers working on its industrialization and another .5 million will be required to finish its current Second Development Plan by 1981. Over two hundred American firms as well as innumerable West German, Japanese, French, Italian, and South Korean firms are fulfilling development contracts in Saudi Arabia as well as throughout the Arab development world.

Therefore, the tasks of constructing, training, and deploying a modern domestic labor force, technological sector, and industrial base have proceeded without the excesses and waste associated with previous forms of industrialization. Although the Arabs are experiencing a heavy dose of "future shock" as their purchases abroad inundate their countries with a torrent of needed and superfluous goods, their developmental social costs up to this point have been very low. The impact of "future shock" on these traditional Islamic cultures should not, of course, be ignored. The "Jeddah syndrome" of transportation bottlenecks, building delays, bureaucratic tie-ups, and general congestion of rapid growth are exacting certain social costs in the Arab developmental model. Yet, these costs usually remain uncalculated because of their chaotic character. Moreover, the fact that industrialization has imposed relatively fewer hardships on the Arab population and class structure is important for understanding their unchanged coalitions of internal social forces and ready acceptance of immediate industrialization. As long as industrial development continues with matching increases in material benefits, it is quite likely the elite coalitions and their developmental designs will continue to hold political power.

Until the 1960s, the Arab states usually portrayed themselves as fellows of the very poor but morally pure Fourth World nations. Together with the African, Asian, and Latin American nations, the Arab states confronted the First World with demands for development aid and assistance to partly redress the economic exploitation which resulted from their unequal exchanges. Yet, as the Arab states have moved into a phase of lessened backwardness, they also have acted economically, diplomatically, and politically, like a group of nouveaux riches. Because of their newfound wealth and status, the Arab states have gradually begun to behave much more like the developed First World states and they are forgetting their former fraternity with the Fourth World nations. As they develop, in other words, the Arab states are displaying sure signs of embourgeoisement.

Embourgeoisement represents the outcome of several political trends. First, and undoubtedly foremost, the Arabs'

economic power since 1971-73 has become awesomely important. The financial solvency of many First World nations is
now dependent upon Arab financial assistance, the developmental future of much of the Fourth World rests upon Arab oil
energy, and the entire economic outlook of the industrialized
nations can be changed radically by decisions made in Arab
capitals. The internal conflicts in OPEC over maintaining the
U.S. dollar as the oil-price currency and over the timing of new
price hikes, which have been stalled for nearly a year, illustrate
the careful regard that the OPEC states have for the OECD
region (MEED, 5/16/78:13). This new power has been
accompanied by a cautious, conservative, and more responsible
foreign policy that has less interest in moral purity on the
questions of economic exploitation, unequal exchange, or
underdevelopment because OPEC now can be rightly seen as
partly causing these ills itself. Second, the Arab states' political
"victories" in 1973—both in the October war and the following
oil embargo—have eased their defeat complex vis-à-vis the
First World. They are now the equals and partners of the First
World nations who, in turn, have shown the Arab states that
the new obligations, responsibilities, and behaviors in the
IBRD, IFAD, and IMF that go along with such status do not
easily fit the Arabs' association with Fourth World states. The
Arab radicalism which was possible in the 1950s and 1960s
when the Arabs fought Israel with Western surplus weapons
and African revolutionaries trained in Algeria's old FLN
(Front de Libération Nationale) camps is no longer affordable
as the Arabs spend billions on advanced arms and industrial
development. In the 1970s, the new Third World Arab states
have developed to the point that they now have much to lose
unless they behave with restraint and caution. And third, the
Arabs' embourgeoisement draws heavily from their mode of
development. Transnational oil corporations served as the
main model for Arab organization and policy as these states
embarked upon economic development. The clearly bourgeois
institutions of international finance and trade, transnational
oil production, and industrial planning and management are
the Arabs' prime fields of action in the 1970s. This institutional
base affords infertile ground for Fourth World radical politics.

Saudi Arabia, for example, has maintained the hard-nosed line of the IMF, rather than the generous stance of Arab fraternity, on refinancing Sudan's severely troubled economy. Worried about Sudan's $2 billion in foreign debts—$800 million of it to Saudi Arabia—the Saudis' have balked at loaning the Sudanese another $700 million without first exacting strict austerity measures from the latter (MEED, 5/19/78:15).

As newly wealthy states, the Arab countries are reproducing many of the dependency relations they once suffered under, but now are themselves the beneficiaries of the economic dependence. The Arab states are striving to assert themselves hegemonically over the Fourth World, especially in Africa, through international aid programs, petroleum price-relief programs, and moral leadership at international summits. In the Fourth World, the Arabs seek higher prices on their oil, but low prices on Fourth World exports. Fearing an OPEC-like price hike by the International Bauxite Association against their budding aluminum industries, five Arab OPEC states and Egypt are negotiating a $1 billion joint venture with Guinea to assure a steady and cheap supply of bauxite (MEED, 1/20/78:10). Consequently, the current-account balances of the NODCs have a deficit of $26.5 billion largely due to increased Arab oil prices (*Banker,* 1977:92). The Arab OPEC states have returned little to the non-Islamic NODCs for expropriating an estimated 2.5 percent of the NODCs' GNP from 1974 through 1977. Indeed, when the Arab states do make investments in the Fourth World, they seek guarantees from the host nations *against* the nationalization or sequestration of their assets— ironically, this requirement is standard operating procedure at the Saudi Development Fund (*Arab Economist,* 1977:23). The African and Asian nations are being "decapitalized" by high Arab oil prices; in 1974 the NODCs received $11.3 billion in developmental assistance, but their oil bills increased at the same time by $11 billion (Blair, 1976:274). At the same time, "indirectly a large share of the OPEC surplus was channeled to more credit-worthy countries via the international banking system" (OECD 1976:41) as the African and Asian MSAs went without effective aid relief from the Arab OPEC states.

The Fourth World is becoming more closely tied to the Third World because of Arab oil and petrochemical imports. Yet, at the same time, the Arab countries are not investing in the destitute Fourth World area. In breaking out of many of their old dependency relations, the Arab OPEC states have placed much of Africa and Asia into new sets of asymmetrical dependency cycles. The Arab states' embourgeoisement denies their membership in the planet's "Southern" camp; rather it indicates that the Arab OPEC countries are the latest and most enthusiastic initiates of the "Northern" region.

7
The Arabs and Africa:
A Changing Relationship

The New Situation

In this study, three related sets of propositions have been argued. (1) The era of Afro-Arab solidarity, widely hailed by statesmen and scholars alike, turns out to have been relatively short-lived, having run its course in little over ten years. The era began when Arab political arguments gained the additional merit of being supplemented by enormous economic leverage, and appears to be moving to an end as it becomes clear that the price of that solidarity for the Africans is much higher than they had expected. (2) The principal factor in the deterioration of Afro-Arab relations has been a basic shift in the international status and mobility of the Arab states. Led by their oil-producing states, the Arabs have, in effect, "moved to a better part of town," leaving their former friends behind and taking on the behavior of their new, rich neighbors. As we demonstrated, these states have become part of a new Third World, sharing not the general impoverishment and political-economic disadvantages of the old Third World, but the vested interests and international outlook of the First and Second Worlds. (3) The Arab shift has left erstwhile African friends much worse off than they were before the new era dawned (ca. 1967), turning them into clients and/or dependents where they once had been equals and leaving them doubly vulnerable to political and economic changes in the international environment.

If, as has been argued, the Arab OPEC states—the core of

OPEC itself—have moved onto a different developmental plane and effectively become members of a new Third World, the African non-oil-producing states have very little to look forward to. To be sure, they will continue to receive various forms of aid from the Arabs, be it bilateral or through multilateral channels of exclusively Arab or international inspiration such as the IMF, the IBRD, or the IDA—the IBRD's soft-loan facility. They will also benefit from the OECD's Financial Support Fund, OPEC's own Special Fund (to which $1.6 billion was committed for 1976 and 1977), and other agencies to which Arab states have made contributions (AFDB, ADF, etc.).

The point made earlier, and to which we now return, is that notwithstanding such assistance, most African countries—and in particular the MSAs—have scarcely begun to recover from the situation created by the oil crisis at the end of 1973. The oil-price explosion—immediately followed by a sharp rise in the cost of imported manufactures—slashed the payment surpluses of the strongest African states, threw the marginal nations into debt, and pushed some into virtual bankruptcy. Africa's rate of growth before the oil crisis averaged 5.6 percent but was cut to 3.8 percent by December 1976. The poorest countries, the so-called basket cases, were only able to achieve a growth rate of 2 percent which, allowing for an average population growth of 2.8 percent, means a negative real growth of 0.8 percent (ARB/ETF, 1976:3889; see also West, 1974). It also has become much harder for African countries to borrow on the Eurodollar market, particularly since Zaire's default on its interest payments in 1975, and when they do it is at very high interest rates and for only relatively short terms. Further, private investment in Africa has slowed down considerably, except, of course, in the oil-producing African states of Nigeria and Gabon plus a few select countries with brighter prospects such as the Ivory Coast and Cameroon.

From the perspective of the African MSAs, the outlook seems almost unrelievedly bleak, and it is hardly surprising that African frustrations came to the surface following the December 1976 OPEC price increase and at the Afro-Arab Summit in March 1977; they are also reflected through increased African use of the threat to re-establish relations with Israel and abandon the new alliance (ARB/ETF, 1977:4124-24, 4190-91).

It is doubtful that either expressions of anger or the threat to shift position on Arab-Israeli issues will serve to loosen Arab purse strings or to persuade the Arabs that their future lies with their former friends. Neither has done so thus far, nor, indeed, have repeated invocations of Third World solidarity, fraternity, and friendship. Not even Nigeria, sub-Saharan Africa's biggest oil producer and now the second most important source of U.S. imported oil, could be persuaded to sell oil at concessional prices to its African neighbors, though it did at one time offer cheaper oil to African states with refineries provided they did not resell it below the fixed OPEC price. Nothing came of the offer, and, in fact, Nigeria has consistently opposed a two-tier pricing system (Aluko, 1976:425).

The realities of the situation are not hard to discern. For Nigeria and Gabon, both members of OPEC, departing from the OPEC line would mean (1) undermining the common front that has been OPEC's strength thus far, (2) a possible loss of revenue precisely when it is needed most to help their own development plans—it is often forgotten that Nigeria is OPEC's second most populous country— and (3) the prospect of being left adrift in the treacherous currents of international competition. Moreover, other African countries now producing oil in useful quantities, such as Angola, Congo, and Zaire, or those with encouraging prospects for bringing in new oil, such as Cameroon and the Ivory Coast, have said nothing on the subject and are not expected to (Wright, 1977:45-47).

For the Arabs, the Africans' threat comes too late to be effective. To begin with, the connection between the oil-price rise and the politics of the Arab-Israeli conflict was fortuitous at best; the precipitous rise actually began *before* the October war, and that conflict simply provided the excuse to do quickly what the Arabs had intended all along to do more gradually. Once firmly in the Arab camp, and once becoming heavily indebted to the Arabs as African economies deteriorated, the Africans' threat to shift position on the Arab-Israeli dispute could do very little to affect their situation.

Even if every African country in economic difficulty were to resume relations with Israel tomorrow, or the Arab-Israeli dispute were to be settled the day after, the basic difficulties of the African non-oil-producing states would remain the same. They will remain dependent on OPEC oil, their development plans will remain in shambles, and their trade balances will continue in net deficit (Kenen, 1975).

Most unfortunate, however, for the position of the African LDCs is the fact that the Arab-Israeli dispute has lost some of its importance for the Arab-African relationship. Given the Arab OPEC states' new preoccupation with internal development, with prudent investment in the West and elsewhere, and with the management of their new international position, African support on Arab-Israeli questions is no longer as vital to them as it once was. The OPEC Arabs have made their point, so to speak, and now consider the First World much more important to the realization of their economic and political goals than the old Third World. Evidence for the new emphasis is not hard to find; it includes, for example, the informal alliance between the United States and Saudi Arabia, and, not surprisingly, the complaints by the so-called confrontation states—Egypt, Syria, and Jordan—that the wealthy Arab oil producers, in the words of the official Damascus daily *Al-Baath*, have "accumulated illegitimate wealth at the expense of the martyrs of the October [1973] war" (MEED, 4/3/77:13). In sum, the African states must now reconcile themselves to the fact that despite the rhetoric of the Afro-Arab Summit, they have become largely peripheral to the very issue that brought them and the Arabs together. They must now fend for themselves as part of the larger group of the new Fourth World states, seeking relief for their troubles from the First, Second, and new Third Worlds.

Points of Conflict

The new realities now also encompass a number of situations of open confrontation containing elements of real or potentially corrosive Arab-African antagonism. The continuing Eritrean-Ethiopian and Western Saharan conflicts, the 1978 Ethiopian-Somali war, and the undeclared war between Chad and Libya have all served to undermine the Arab-African connection and once again raise in African minds old fears about the motives and intentions of the Arab states.

Given the nature of the vital national interests engaged in these situations, there is no way of knowing if Arab-African confrontation could have been avoided in each case or if the recent deterioration of the Arab-African alliance contributed to the evolution of the situations themselves. However, this much can be said: where fundamental Arab and African interests clash, the alliance—and all the goodwill it implies—has had little or no restraining effect on those involved. A look at key aspects of the Ethiopian-Somali war and summary glances at the war in Chad and the Western Saharan situation help to make the point.

There is no need to rehearse here the basic facts about the Ethiopian-Somali war, which began, to all intents and purposes, when elements of the Somali army joined the drive mounted by the guerillas of the Western Somali Liberation Front (WSLF) during the latter part of 1977, and which ended on March 9, 1978, when Somalia announced that it would withdraw its forces from Ethiopia's Ogaden region. In the interim, the Soviet Union had completed its switch of support from the Somalis to the Ethiopians, and Soviet-equipped and Cuban-led Ethiopian units had decisively routed the combined Somali-WSLF forces in and around Jijiga, the key to control of the Ogaden. What is of interest here is not the war itself but the complicated set of international alignments and support networks evoked by the conflict, some of which placed Arab states on opposing sides, others of which put African states in opposition, and still others which opposed Africans to Arabs.

Again, it was the crucial interests involved that determined the configurations of external support. The stakes were simple enough for the Ethiopians and the Somalis. The Ethiopians sought to retain possession of the Ogaden and Haud regions which, though the object of an old dispute with Somalia, had been under the generally recognized control of the preceding regime of Haile Selassie. (Two good summaries of the dispute are Drysdale, 1964, and Bell, 1973.) The Somalis had long claimed the Ogaden and Haud as part of a Somalia irredenta, and apparently saw in Ethiopia's mounting internal turmoil the opportunity to take by force what had been denied them at the negotiating table.

Iraq, Syria, and the PLO gave the Somalis open diplomatic and material support, mainly because of what they contended was pan-Arab and ideological solidarity with Somalia's socialist regime. Egypt, North Yemen, the United Arab Emirates, and Saudi Arabia provided similar support, ostensibly on behalf of their versions of pan-Arab and pan-Islamic solidarity but much more clearly because of a desire to assure security in the Red Sea, that is, prevent radical Marxist and pro-Soviet regimes from controlling access to the Red Sea, the Straits of Bab el Mandeb, and the Gulf of Aden. Jordan, though it provided no material aid to Somalia, joined Egypt and the others for much the same reasons. Morocco, Mauritania, and Tunisia declared support for Somalia because of pan-Arab motives and because of their anti-Soviet attitudes. Algeria officially took no sides, nor did the Arab League. Most of the League's members were sympathetic to the Somalis, but the organization itself refrained from taking a definite stand because it wished to prevent internal schisms and to avoid upsetting Arab-African cooperation. South Yemen and Libya proclaimed their neutrality toward the conflict, but they hardly bothered to conceal either their sympathies for Ethiopia or the fact that they provided financial, logistical, and technical assistance to the Ethiopian regime. South Yemen most probably acted on the basis of its close ties to the Soviet Union, and Libya undoubtedly did so because of its hostility to the regimes in Saudi Arabia, Egypt, and the Sudan. (The Numeiry government is close to the Sadat regime, has equivocated over the conflict in the Horn, supported Eritrean secession, and taken anti-Soviet stances; *Jeune Afrique,* cited in ARB/PSC, 1978:4740-41.)

The Africans, for their part, also had to contend with sets of conflicting motives and interests. First, it should be remembered that most African governments consider Somalis as Africans, despite Somalia's membership in the Arab League and the Somali leadership's self-proclaimed Arabness. Somalia was a founding member of the Organization of African Unity, as was Ethiopia, where the seat of the organization is located. It is probably fair to summarize the position of the majority of African states as regretfully tilting toward Ethiopia, despite the fact that the Mengitsu regime enjoyed little support and even less sympathy on the continent. At stake, for most African states, was a basic principle enshrined in the OAU charter itself, that is, the inviolability of African frontiers. Indifference, or even support for Somalia, would have meant flinging back the lid of the Pandora's box of territorial claims already pried ajar by the Libyans in Chad, by the Moroccans and Mauritanians in the Western Sahara, and by Idi Amin's occasional demands for his neighbors' border areas. The OAU, unwilling to offend Arab sensibilities or endanger Arab-African cooperation, confronted the matter in oblique fashion. On January 20, 1978, it warned Iran, which was providing financial and military aid to Somalia, against seeking to extend its sphere of influence in Africa and, more significantly, called on "foreign powers" to "stop meddling in African affairs as regards the present conflict in the Horn of Africa" (ARB/PSC, 1978:4702). The warning, seen in context, appears not only as direct rebuke to Iran, but also as an appeal to all the other states—notably Arab ones—who were rendering direct assistance to the Somalis.

The Kenyans, one of the proximate neighbors to the conflict, have been much clearer and more direct on the issue. What makes the Kenyan reaction significant is not only Kenya's closeness to the conflict and its direct stake in the outcome, but the fact that on Arab-African issues Kenya often articulates what other African states hesitate to say themselves. Thus, it is hardly surprising that the Kenyans, Somalia's southern neighbors and frequent targets of Somali irredentist activity, should have felt threatened by the 1978 Ethiopian-Somali war. What was unexpected was Kenya's insistence on identifying Somalia as an Arab state and then launching highly charged attacks on *both* Somalia and the Arabs. Kenya's *Daily Nation*, which speaks for the government, has carried numerous articles, letters, and features dealing with Somalia and Arab-African relations. Some sample headlines and topics since 1975 suggest the tenor of the Kenyan commentary: "Jingle bells and oil wells" (poem about Arab oil stinginess, November 29, 1975),

"Somalia slated for map claim on Kenyan land" (article about 1972 Somali map claiming part of Kenya, February 7, 1976), "OAU and national sovereignty" (editorial about "Arab blackmail" and "mischief," July 20, 1976), "Red Sea—a zone of peace?" (editorial worrying about the possibility that the Red Sea might become an "Arab lake," March 24, 1977), "It's time Africa broke ties with the Arab world" (letter, September 6, 1977), "Time to end Somalia's aggression" (editorial, September 7, 1977), "Arab support for Somalia" (*Standard*, February 9, 1978), plus a whole series of articles and editorials in the *Daily Nation* between February 15 and March 6, 1978. Other attacks on the Arab link to the Ethiopian-Somali war include "Cynicism in Arab treatment of Africa" (editorial, *Nairobi Times*, February 19, 1978). Non-Kenyan contributions include: "Arab plot in Africa?" (letter in *Daily Times*, Nigeria, October 8, 1977), and "The Arabs and the Horn of Africa" and "Horn of Africa: Somali Greed" (editorial and lead article in *Afriscope*, September 1977, published in Lagos). The incidents in February 1978 involving unauthorized Egyptian overflights of Kenya and the grounding of an Egyptian plane carrying arms to Somalia—after Egypt had denied it was ferrying arms to Somalia—also served to raise Kenyan hackles further and posed new questions about the Arab-African connection.

While it is true that Somalia also had sympathizers in the African camp (notably Mauritania, which identifies with the Arab League majority), on the whole and despite the unattractiveness of the regime of Addis Ababa, African states appear to have lined up behind the OAU on the issue. Other complications, it should be added, included concern about the Cuban and Soviet roles in the affair (roles endorsed by Angola, Congo, and Mozambique), the "revelation" by Foreign Minister Dayan that Israel had been helping Ethiopia, and the uncomfortable fact that it took "foreign powers" to help settle the matter, if only temporarily, notwithstanding individual African and OAU mediatory efforts. In sum, the war cannot have helped the cause of Arab-African cooperation and may well have undermined the relationship still further.

The Chad-Libyan conflict, while less bloody and complicated than the war on the Horn, also carries serious implications for continued Arab-African harmony. Again, without going into the details of the conflict, the crucial interests can be identified. At stake, briefly, are the following. (1) A strip of Chadian territory varying in width from forty-two to ninety-eight miles—the so-called Aouzou strip comprising some thirty-seven thousand square miles—which includes a substantial part of the Tibesti mountains and where there are said to be important uranium and other mineral deposits. Libya quietly annexed the territory during 1975 and 1976, and, despite Chad's protests at the OAU in 1977 and 1978, had not withdrawn from it by mid-1978. A map issued by the Libyan foreign ministry in 1976 shows the strip as part of Libya, and an even earlier Libyan road map, published in 1970, shows the area included between two sets of frontiers; one, an inner line designated "International boundaries as indicated should not be," and the other, an outer line labeled "Considered authoritative and subject to change." The outer line on the 1970 map becomes the official frontier on the 1976 chart. (2) The future of a rebellion against the Chad government begun twelve years ago during the regime of the late President Tombalbaye and continued against that of his successor, General Félix Malloum. There are at least four main guerilla groups engaged in the rebellion, the most important of which is the Chad National Liberation Front (FROLINAT), largely armed, financed, and supplied openly by the Libyan government. (3) Last, but not least, the physicial survival of the Malloum government. By mid-May 1978, the rebels were in apparent control of the northern two-thirds of the country, and France had to rush in troops and planes, bringing its commitment up to around 1,700 men, to prevent Malloum's forces from being overwhelmed by the rebels (*New York Times*, May 12 and 13, 1978; *Le Monde*, June 13, 1978). Toward the end of May, the French helped repulse a FROLINAT attack on the Chadian garrison at Ati, about 180 miles from Ndjamena, and, a week later, inflicted heavy losses on a large rebel force trapped at Djedda, near Ati.

On March 27, 1978, after Chad was unable to find support at the UN for its complaint—co-sponsored by France—against Libya, Chad signed what was billed as "an act of reconciliation" in which it agreed to recognize FROLINAT, observe a cease-fire, and work toward national reconciliation. The agreement, co-signed by its ostensible guarantors—Sudan, Niger, and Libya—said nothing about the Aouzou strip or about FROLINAT's call (published by its Revolutionary Council on March 16) for the overthrow of the "dictatorial, neocolonial regime imposed by France since August 11, 1960," and an end to "imperialist interference" in Chad (ARB/PSC, 1978:4780-81). Under the circumstances, the "cease-fire" looked more like a capitulation. On April 30, FROLINAT denounced all parts of the agreement, and the war went on. However, neither FROLINAT reverses in June, nor the co-option of one of the rebel leaders (Hissene Habre) into the Malloum regime as prime minister in early September, has yet served to defuse the conflict.

The March 27 agreement was signed in Benghazi, Libya. Libya was and continues to be the prime support of FROLINAT—and probably of other groups as well—supplying it with cash, headquarters, training facilities, sanctuary and secure bases, and weapons up to and including artillery, armored vehicles, and surface-to-air missiles. Libyan troops continue to occupy the Aouzou strip, and Chad has charged that Libyan regulars have assisted rebel troops in Chad itself. In all, there is ample justification for designating the conflict as an undeclared war, and for suggesting that even though the OAU has been reticent to condemn Libya for its actions, the situation is bound to affect African confidence in the Arab states' intentions toward their African neighbors.

Finally, a few words about the Western Saharan conflict. Ever since the tripartite agreement of November 14, 1975, in which Spain handed over its rights to the Western Sahara (then known as the Spanish Sahara) to Morocco and Mauritania, those two countries have been fighting a war against the guerillas of the Popular Front for the Liberation of Saguia el Hamra and Río de Oro (Polisario), who are fully backed by neighboring Algeria. By mid-1978 the Polisario had succeeded in tying down sizable elements of the Moroccan army, had forced Mauritania to increase its army from 1,800 to 20,000 men (Hodges, 1978), had raided both Mauritania's iron-ore center,

Zouerate, and its capital, Nouakchott, and had brought French planes and military advisers into the action (Junqua, 1978). Finally, the military coup d'etat which, on July 10, 1978, brought down the twenty-year-old regime of President Mokhtar Ould Daddah, was triggered mainly by the damaging effects of the conflict on Mauritania's economic and political well-being. The primary stakes in this conflict are perhaps easier to identify than those in Chad and the Horn: possession and exploitation of one of the world's largest deposits of phosphates at Bou Craa. Morocco and Mauritania apparently hoped to share the bounty alone and, as a consequence, did not include Algeria in the agreement with Spain. Beyond the phosphates, as Edward Mortimer points out (1978:11-12), lies a danger to King Hassan, who successfully exploited the Western Saharan irredentist issue to build support for the Moroccan monarchy. The conflict also has obvious implications for Mauritania's security and stability, and a "larger, more powerful Morocco buttressed by a docile Mauritanian ally constitutes a geographical threat to Algeria" (Mortimer, 1978:11).

Both sides have mounted intense diplomatic campaigns on behalf of their positions. Morocco and Mauritania have found support from several of the francophone African states, notably Senegal and Zaire. (Morocco, it will be recalled, provided troops to help Zaire repel the 1977 Shaba invasion and to police the province after another invasion in 1978.) On the other hand, Angola, Mozambique, Guinea-Bissau, Benin, Togo, Rwanda, Burundi, Madagascar, and the Seychelles have declared full support for the Saharoui cause and therewith, by implication, for Algeria's interests in the conflict. Given the lineup of countries on both sides and the explosiveness of the issues, it is hardly surprising that the OAU has been unable to find either venues or participants for a special summit on the Western Sahara demanded by Algeria and mandated by the organization in 1976. The latest attempt, by Gabon, to host the summit in Libreville during March 1978 failed because only seven of Africa's forty-nine heads of state accepted the invitation to attend and a quorum of twenty-five was required. The extraordinary summit had earlier been proposed for

Lusaka (Zambia), then Addis Ababa (Ethiopia), and then Cairo. Each proposed site was rejected for financial or security reasons, or because some member states said they would boycott certain venues. The July 1978 OAU Summit Conference in Khartoum also had to deal with the conflict. Once again, in the face of strenuous Algerian objections, the OAU did little more than repeat its call for the special summit and appoint a committee to study the situation—and report in a year's time.

These three points of open conflict are the most visible of the several areas of current Arab-African antagonism. The Chad and Western Saharan situations were still unresolved by mid-1978; the Ethiopian-Somali war, at least its large-scale phase, had ended with the Somali withdrawal of March 9, 1978, leaving the basic issues unsettled and the Somalis returning to guerilla warfare in the Ogaden. The Eritrean-Ethiopian conflict, and its complicated confrontational networks, remains a source of continuing tension, as do Uganda and the Sudan—where the old North-South, ethno-religious antagonisms still simmer. African displeasure with the Arabs now also includes, as was noted earlier, the fact of barely concealed Arab trade, investment, and contact with South Africa.

Implications of the New Situation

If our analysis is correct, the new situation has created dangerous rifts in the Arab-African alliance, rifts severe enough to cause its disintegration. By mid-1978, however, most African states had not taken the steps that would lead to an irreversible breach, opting instead to maintain the form, if not the spirit, of the alliance. The OAU's vacillations in the face of the conflicts discussed above is a good indication of that attitude. So, too, the Arabs; though particular Arab countries have paid but scant attention to African sensitivities, where some conflict engaged their vital political interests, neither the Arab League nor the informal league of Arab oil bankers has moved openly to denounce the alliance. We think that three sets of both short-run and long-term considerations dictate such a stance.

1. In the short run, African states will benefit from continuing, if increasingly parsimonious, aid from OPEC, the

Arab League, and various bilateral Arab-African arrangements. Though aid to the African LDC states—and this now
includes increasing military assistance—comes primarily from
Europe and the DAC countries, North America, and non-Arab
international agencies, the Arab component remains and is
likely to remain an important prop to their troubled
economies.

2. In the long term, the alliance, or at least the appearance of
the alliance, remains useful in preserving nominal unity on
behalf of the global redistributive demands voiced at UNCTAD,
at the Special UN Session in 1975, and in other international
forums. The Arab-African link permits the formulation of a
common line on these problems, the operation of a common
front that magnifies exponentially the limited power of the
African LDC states. Algeria, for example, played an out-
standing role in this connection and in the "Group of 77," as
well as at the Fourth Conference on Non-Aligned Countries
held in its capital (Bouvier, 1974). "No Black country," argues
Alard von Schack, "can fail to recognize that a break with the
African Arabs would lead to serious repercussions—precisely
for the great number of the poorest among them—in the work
of these bodies" (1977:117). This applies also to the work of the
ECA, the CCTA, and certainly the OAU itself. We think it
likely that the real glue that still holds Africans and Arabs
together—however tenuously—is precisely the possible benefits for the Africans that the alliance could have in restructuring
the world economy. However, if this analysis is correct, such
calculation implies increasingly costly long-term hope for
countries which, because of their severe economic problems,
must almost necessarily live in the dangerous, short-term
present.

3. So long as the Arab states maintain the dominant position
in the relationship and the African states appear unwilling—or
are unable—to dispense with its forms, there is no reason for
the Arabs to do so either. If the alliance continues to provide
low-cost benefits to the Arabs, such as a free hand in conflicts
affecting African interests and votes in international organizations, there is every good reason to avoid an open break. Above
all, the alliance has done nothing to impede, and appears in

fact to second, the basic long-term aims of the Arab states.

Insofar as the Arab die has been cast, the oil-producing Arab states and Iran have cast it. Our analysis indicates that their strategic, long-term interests lie with the industrialized West and North America, at home, and with their proximate Arab neighbors, and in a peaceful environment conducive to producing maximum benefits from both their domestic and foreign investments. African MSA and NODC countries argue—ideology and political rhetoric aside—that it is also in the long-term interest of the Arabs to help African development because investment in Africa is the key to the unrealized economic potential of the continent—and to future Arab profits. Arab actions do not suggest that the African argument has been very persuasive; economic relations between the Arab OPEC countries and the African NODCs have tended—with mitigating exceptions being the Muslim or mainly Muslim African states—to emphasize caution, distributive parsimony, and, all too often, barely concealed exploitation. And there isn't much the African NODCs can do about it, at least in the short run.

Final Reflections

A variety of forces have had a hand in building OPEC's new economic and political capabilities. To be sure, the major element of OPEC's strength can be found in the high-energy industrial forms of the OECD nations. The entire post–World War II development in Europe, Japan, and North America was predicated upon readily accessible and fairly cheap energy supplies increasingly taken from petroleum instead of coal. Initially, nationally based oil companies provided a concrete mediation among the oil-producing areas in Africa, Asia, Latin America, and the Middle East. Backed by substantial military power as well as quasi-colonial native administrations, these oil companies maintained a steady supply and acceptable price of petroleum for the oil-consuming nations. Yet, as the quantities of imported petroleum increased almost exponentially, the formerly national oil companies underwent a considerable qualitative transformation. The enlarged dependence of the oil-consuming nations upon the oil-producing nations led to the increasing independence of the oil corporations. They became transnational in both their policy and their loyalty, and their freedom of action, in turn, provided a highly suggestive developmental model for the oil-producing states.

The recent "trilateral" concept is a necessary and direct consequence of the "OPEC" concept. The policy-planning and coordinating model copied from the transnational corporations by the OPEC nations emerges, in turn, in 1973 among the OECD nations. Here, once again, the hitherto unrecognized powers of the transnational corporate form were acknowledged in political practice. In an effort to offset the success of the TNC form—now embroiled in OPEC—the OECD states sought to create an opposing political bloc. The same necessity that prompted the major oil-producing nations to organize against the great petrochemical multinational corporations now asserts itself among the oil-consuming states. Such organization, it must be remembered, has a twofold objective, that is, to deal more effectively with both the transnational corporations and the opposing bloc of states.

The ultimate reality of petroleum "realpolitik" rests in the formation of a new developmental world in the global economic system. Just as the Second, or Communist, world emerged from a cataclysm—the Bolshevik Revolution—for the First World, the emergence of this new world has already shaken the industrialized West down to its deepest economic roots. In the process, the new developmental world of OPEC states gained immense new international prestige, political leverage, and economic clout. These trends manifest themselves in the massive transfer of wealth from one bloc to another, in the new international reference group of the OPEC nations, in the economic prosperity of their national economies, and in the creation of the new international tier below them. The OPEC states, in the eyes of OECD and the East European Communist states, are no longer the brethren of Bolivia, Kenya, Burma, or Afghanistan. On the contrary, their new political and economic capabilities, both those already tested and those yet promised, make them the equals of North

America, Europe, Japan, the Soviet Union, and China.

New developmental worlds differentiate themselves through catastrophe. The catastrophic rite of passage propels them out of their former low estate and into a new international tier of their own making. Collective activity accomplished through common will along unprecedented political paths demonstrates their economic capacity, organizational integrity, and political ability. For the OPEC bloc, it was no mean feat to become an international powerhouse, banker, and potential workshop, all against the resistance of transnational corporations and the industrialized West.

We do not argue that the new OPEC developmental world will last forever, or that some new cataclysm may not once again transform the international status system. We do argue that so long as oil continues as the world's prime strategic commodity, the new Third World will continue to benefit from the massive forced capital redistribution that has been the principal effect of its creation. We may, perhaps, even be on the verge of a new economic imperialism in which the relatively rich First and Second World states contribute to the coffers of the new Third World, be it directly through capital transfers, or indirectly, as aid from the First and Second Worlds funnels through the new Fourth World and emerges as payments for oil, interest on loans, and commodity exchanges or as capital flight. The poor states, of which the African LDCs are the most numerous, will thus have become the unwilling dependents of both the old First and the new Third Worlds. Unless the states of the old First World find ways of altering the emerging pattern to their own and the new Fourth World's benefit, it is at best an unpleasant prospect.

Appendixes

Note

The documents and other materials appended here were selected to complement and illustrate the arguments in this book. The quotation from Nasser's *Philosophy of the Revolution* and the excerpts from an interview with Senegal's President Senghor exemplify views about Arab-African relations that were once commonly held by Arab and African leaders. The editorial from Kenya's *Daily News* is an example of the extent to which favorable views about the Arab world had deteriorated by the mid-1970s, even though the official collective position (as witnessed by the OAU resolutions) remained fixed on a stance of complete support for Arab causes. The Cairo Declaration, announced at the 1977 Afro-Arab summit, represents the attempt to formalize and reinforce the Arab-African connection which, by that time, had begun to unravel. The last appendix lists, in accessible tabular form, the various Arab financial institutions frequently mentioned in the text.

Appendix A:
President Nasser of Egypt
on Arab-African Relations

As for the Second Circle—the African Continent Circle I should say, without going into details, that we cannot under any condition, even if we wanted to, stand aloof from the terrible and terrifying battle now raging in the heart of that continent between five million whites and two hundred million Africans.

We cannot stand aloof for one important and obvious reason—we ourselves are in Africa.

Surely the people of Africa will continue to look to us—we who are the guardians of the Continent's northern gate—we who constitute the connecting link between the Continent and the outer world.

We certainly cannot, under any conditions, relinquish our responsibility to help spread the light of knowledge and civilisation to the very depth of the virgin jungles of the Continent . . .[9]

There still remains one more reason—the beloved Sudan, whose boundaries extend to the heart of the Continent where it is bound by neighbourly relations, being the sensitive centre.[10]

It is undeniable that Africa is now the scene of a strange and stirring commotion. The white man, who represents several European nations, is again trying to change the map of the Continent. We cannot under any condition stand as mere onlookers, deluding ourselves into believing we are in no way

Source: Gamal Abdel Nasser. *Philosophy of the Revolution.* Cairo: The National Publications House, 1954. Pp. 69-70.

117

concerned with these machinations.

Indeed, I shall continue to dream of the day on which I shall
see in Cairo a great African Institute seeking to reveal to us the
various aspects of the Continent, to create in our minds an
enlightened African consciousness, and to associate itself with
all those working in all parts of the world for the progress,
prosperity and welfare of the peoples of Africa.

Appendix B:
President Leopold Sedar Senghor of Senegal on African-Arab Relations and the Middle East Conflict

Q: Mr. President, Arab-Africans and Negro-Africans also misunderstand each other politically. For example, Negro-Africans don't feel the same way about the Palestinian drama as they do about the struggle for independence in southern Africa.

A: Why? Because the facts are not seen as they really are. Often, the problems are poorly defined. The Middle East? Some say it is a racial issue. *Yet Jews and Arab-Berbers are* [both] *Semites! Is it a religious question? Be it Islam, Judaism, or Christianity—we are all the heirs of Abraham.* The issue is basically political. In Senegal, we see the problem thus: *there is a conflict, not between Jews and Muslims, but between Israel and the Arab States.* [The conflict] concerns colonization, the occupation of land, the right of the first occupant. Since the problem is basically political, it must be seen from a political point of view.

What are the political facts? There are about 100 million Arabs in the world, of which 80 million are African [and] represented in the Organization of African Unity. Therefore, it is as members of the O.A.U. that we should study the elements of the problem and the situation with the Arabs. We do not say that the Arabs are right *a priori,* but we must go to the Arabs to study the situation with them, to see where they are right and where they are wrong, and to try, with them, to settle the problem peacefully.

Source: "Noirs, Arabes, Juifs" [Blacks, Arabs, Jews], *Continent 2,000* 2 (November 1969):3-14. Translation from the French by V. T. Le Vine. (Italics in the original.)

119

It is in this sense that I have always demanded—and I've given the same instructions this year—that our representatives at the UN insist that the African group of states take up the problem before the start of each General Assembly.

We want to remind the African group of our solidarity, and without aligning ourselves exactly with [the Arabs], we want to aid our Arab brethren in their analysis of the problem after having analyzed it with them. . . .

This morning I again spoke with the Israeli ambassador. I said to him, we have not broken with Israel. We agree on the goal of attaining, that is to say, of guaranteeing the independence of all states in the region, within the limits of their frontiers. [To this end] we must use all available paths to a settlement. On the other hand, I added, I don't agree with all the means being used. We think that negotiations should be conducted under the aegis of the United Nations and that it is the United Nations, in particular the great powers, who should guarantee the new frontiers without thereby also consecrating (the results of) conquest. As I told him, *if the problem is political, it also has a religious aspect, and that is Jerusalem, because Jerusalem concerns not only the Israelis. Jerusalem* [also] *concerns a billion Christians and 600 million Muslims.*

In any case, this is how we in Senegal have tried to enlighten public opinion without [also fostering] hate because, beyond the conflict itself, *there is the historic and prehistoric solidarity of long-suffering peoples, what I call the trilogy of suffering peoples—the Jews, the Arabs, and the Blacks.* And I said to the Israeli ambassador that I hoped that after the peaceful settlement of the conflict, there could be cooperation among these suffering peoples.

Q: How can the Negro-African states help in solving the Palestinian problem?

A: The African delegations together must examine the facts of the problem, [must] define a common stand before the General Assembly, all with the aim of reaching positive solutions that can resolve the problem. What is involved is obtaining the withdrawal of Israeli troops from Arab territories and finding a definitive solution by recognizing the existence of all states in the region. . . . Moreover, I think that if the Middle East problem is not yet solved, if the Nigerian problem is not yet solved, it is because we do not have a clear sense of these problems, because we lack the dynamic will to reach positive solutions. In these situations, the fault is much less that of the UN than it is of the African governments themselves.

Appendix C:
Editorial: Arabs, Jews and Africans

When Arab nations surprised the world with an oil embargo, they made promises to the Organisation of African Unity in this connection. The first was that Africans were, of course, brothers, and that arrangements would be made for the African continent to receive oil from the Arabs, and to increase their volume of trade with the Arabs.

Now, what did Africa get in return? An agreement was signed between the Secretary-General of the Organisation of African Unity and a company called the London and Rhodesia Company to the effect that it would act as a middle-agent and supply all Africa's oil needs. After considerable argument, the agreement was abrogated for very good reasons—a strategic material such as oil could not be left in the hands of one foreign company.

After that, African nations were to experience a high rate of inflation caused by the oil embargo in the way of costly imported raw and finished materials—and yet the Arab nations did not either increase their volume of trade or aid to compensate Africans for the oil price rise induced inflation. Instead, most of the Arab aid has been going to Islamic nations and into the Jihad fund administered by Libya's Col. Gaddafi.

Central to this deception was the proposition that the problem of South Africa as it concerns the rest of Africa is identical with the problem of Israel as that State concerns the Arab world. You scratch our backs, so spake the Arabs, and

Source: Editorial in Kenya *Daily Nation*, July 20, 1976.

we'll scratch yours. In other words, give us support against Israel, and we will give you support against South Africa.

In the first place, this equation, again, does not hold. Left to themselves, Africans and South Africans can settle their own problems. After all, Africans acknowledge the right of White South Africans to live in peace, and accept a constitutional settlement to the colour bar there.

In contradistinction to this stance by Africa, the Arabs do not accept the right of Israel to exist. The final solution to the Israel question, they say, is the dismemberment of Israel and dispersion of the Jews. The least one can say about this sorry scheme of things is that the Israeli/Arab quarrel is not an African issue—and Africa should be kept out of it. The most that one can say about it is that Israel as a nation State has the right to exist, and Africans must not be party to a complicity to destroy a people. That is against natural justice.

Since the breaking of relations with Israel was based on falsehood, deception and chicanery, and time has proved this point, is it not time that African States resumed relations with Israel, with the resolution that never again will they be deceived into precipitate action based on whims and emotions?

Resumption of relations with Israel by African nations will at least restore some confidence which has been shattered by such erratic statements as the ones which have spewed forth from President Amin's mouth—utterances which are as incoherent and execrable as the very sight of the River Nile after massacres in Uganda and a great overflowing.

Appendix D:
Typical Resolutions on Middle East
Questions Passed by the OAU

On the Middle East and Occupied Arab Territories
AHG/Res. 76 (XII)

The Assembly of Heads of State and Government of the OAU: having heard the statements delivered during the Session of the Council of Ministers by the representatives of the Arab Republic of Egypt and the PLO and other delegations, having received the report of the OAU Administrative Secretary-General (CM/660 and 660 Add. I [XXV]), recalling resolutions AHG/Res. 67 (IX), AHG/Res. 70 (X), CM/Res. 332 (XXIII), as well as resolution CM/Res. 393 (XXIV), and the declaration concerning Palestine and the Middle East, CM/ST. 14 (XXIV), guided by the principles and objectives of the Charter of the OAU and the UN and by the common destiny of the Arab and African peoples, as well as their continuous struggle for their rights, freedom, peace and independence, noting with deep concern the constant deterioration of the situation in the Middle East as a result of Israel's persistent policy of aggression and refusal to abide by the UN resolutions, together with its continued aggression on the Arab people within and outside the occupied Arab territories, and its continuous obstruction of every effort to achieve a just and durable peace, with the aim of gaining time and imposing a fait-

Source: Executive Secretariat, Organization of African Unity, Addis Ababa, Ethiopia. Reprinted in Colin Legum, Ed., *Africa Contemporary Record, Annual Survey and Documents 1975-76.* New York: Africana, 1976. Pp. C18-C20.

accompli to establish aggression and occupation, reaffirming that just and permanent peace in Palestine and the Middle East can only be attained on the basis of complete Israeli withdrawal from all the occupied Arab territories and the exercise by the Palestinians of their full national rights to sovereignty, national independence and self-determination; asserting that continued Israeli occupation of Arab lands by force and violation of the national rights of the Palestinian people are, in themselves, a continued aggression and a serious threat to the security, the territorial integrity and the sovereignty of Arab countries and peoples, deeply concerned by the invalidity and illegitimacy of the measures taken by Israel to alter the human, geographical and cultural features in the occupied Arab territories with the aid of Judaization of Jerusalem and other parts of the occupied Arab territories, convinced that owing to Israel's continued violation of the principles of the UN Charter and its continued aggression against Arab countries and the Palestinian people, it is time to apply the sanctions stipulated by the Charter of the UN against Israel, further convinced of the necessity for the OAU to adopt adequate and practical measures to confront the Zionist enemy's continued aggression and violation:

1. Reaffirms its total and effective support for the frontline States and the Palestinian people in their legitimate struggle to restore all the occupied territories and usurped rights by every possible means;

2. Condemns Israel's policy of aggression, expansion, and annexation of Arab territories by force, and its attempts to alter their demographic, geographic, economic and cultural features;

3. Condemns Israel's continued refusal to abide by the resolutions of the UN and its deliberation, obstruction, by all means of manoeuvring, of every effort exerted to establish a just and permanent peace in the area;

4. Further condemns the persistent policy of repression pursued by Israeli occupation authorities against Arab inhabitants in the occupied Arab territories, as well as its persistent violation of their human rights, and its violation of the 1949 Geneva Convention, in particular the Fourth,

concerning the protection of civilian inhabitants, and its barbaric attacks and raids on refugee camps and bombardment of civilian targets in the towns and villages of Southern Lebanon in violation of all principles of international and human laws;

5. Strongly condemns the attitude of the States supplying Israel with assistance, arms and means of killing and destruction, and holds that the real purpose underlying the flooding of Israel with such enormous quantities of weaponry is to establish it as an advanced base for racism and colonialism in the heart of the Arab and African world and of the Third World, and further considers that any aid or support to Israel is actually an encouragement and a participation in the consolidation of the Israeli occupation and persistent aggression;

6. Reaffirms once more its resolution CM/Res. 20 of the Eighth Extra-Ordinary Session;

7. Invites all African States to extend all possible potentialities available in the African world to the Arab confrontation powers so as to reinforce their struggle against the Zionist aggression;

8. Calls upon all OAU member-States to take the most appropriate measures to intensify pressures exercised against Israel at the UN and other Institutions, including the possibility of eventually depriving it of its status as member of these Institutions;

9. Considers Zionism a danger to world peace, and decides to organize an information campaign in which all African information media participate to unmask the racist aggressive nature of the Zionist entity in a continuous and planned manner, and to confront and refute all Zionist misleading propaganda campaigns aimed at arousing hostility against both the Arab and African Worlds;

10. Requests the OAU Administrative Secretary-General to closely follow up developments in the Middle East and to report thereon to the 26th Session of the Council of Ministers, and decides to keep the situation in the Middle East as one of the important items on the agenda of the next Session of the OAU Council of Ministers.

Reservations:
Sierra-Leone, Senegal, Liberia
Opposition:
Zaire

On the Question of Palestine
AHG/Res. 77 (XII)

The Assembly of Heads of State and Government of the OAU: recalling the resolution adopted by the OAU Council of Ministers at its 24th Ordinary Session held in Addis Ababa from 13-21 February 1975, guided by the principles and provisions of the Charter of the OAU and the UN, and noting with appreciation the heroic sacrifices of the Palestine people in the face of the Zionist aggression for the liberation of Palestine, having studied the developments of the Palestine cause and the grave situation arising from the continued occupation by Israel of Arab territories, its usurpation of the legitimate rights of the Palestine people, its refusal to abide by the UN resolutions in this respect, particularly UN General Assembly Resolution No. 3236 adopted at its 29th Session, its denial of the national rights of the Palestine people in Palestine, including their return to their homeland, their right to recover their property and to self-determination without any foreign intervention, and having likewise condemned the continued Israeli usurpation of Palestine and the dispersal of its people.

Considering that this situation constitutes a flagrant violation of the UN Charter and Resolutions as well as of the Universal Declaration on Human Rights, and that its continuation represents a grave threat to international peace and security, considering that the Palestinian question is the root cause of the struggle against the Zionist enemy, reasserting the legality of the struggle of the Palestine people for the restoration of their full national rights, considering that the racist regime in occupied Palestine and the racist regimes in Zimbabwe and SA have a common imperialist origin, forming a whole and having the same racist structure and being organically linked in their policy aimed at repression of the dignity and integrity of the human being, considering that support of the member-States of the OAU for the people of Palestine in their struggle for the restoration of their national rights in Palestine and for their right to self-determination is a duty imposed by Afro-Arab solidarity;

Expressing its conviction that the military, economic, political and moral support of Israel by a number of States, notably the U.S., enables it to persist in its policy of aggression and to further reinforce its usurpation of Palestine and its occupation of Arab Territories, considering that maintaining relations with Israel in the political, economic, trade, communications and other domains assists it to reinforce its usurpation of Palestine and to persist in its expansionist policy of aggression, considering that the continuation of the membership of Israel in the UN contradicts the principles and Charter of the UN and encourages Israel to ignore UN resolutions and to collude with various racist, expansionist and aggressive regimes,

1. Decides:

(a) to provide full and effective support to the Palestine people in their legitimate struggle to restore their national rights, including:

(i) their right to return to their homeland, Palestine, and to recover their property.

(ii) their right to self-determination without any foreign intervention.

(iii) their right to sovereignty over their territory.

(iv) their right to establish their independent national authority.

(b) to work in all domains to concretize recognition of these rights and ensure respect for them. The member-States of the OAU also undertake to adopt all appropriate measures towards that end;

(c) that the OAU Liberation Committee and the Palestine Liberation Organization should jointly lay down a strategy aiming at liberating Palestine, considering that the cause of Palestine is an African cause;

2. Calls upon all member-States to support the people of Palestine by every means in their struggle against Zionist racist

colonialism to restore their full national rights. Member-States, moreover, assert that restitution of their rights is an essential condition for the establishment of a just and lasting peace in the Middle East;

3. Calls upon the UN to work for the application of Resolution 3236 adopted by the General Assembly at its 29th Session;

4. Reasserts that the Palestine Liberation Organization is the sole legal representative of the Palestine people and their legitimate struggle;

5. Requests member-States to implement the pertinent resolutions of previous OAU Summits and Foreign Ministers' Conferences on the Palestinian Cause as soon as possible;

6. Reiterates that it is desirable, in order to ensure the success of the PLO in its struggle to concretize the future of the Palestinian People's State, to provide it with all facilities and opportunities to intensify its contracts with the governments of member-States;

7. Condemns Israel's violation of human rights in the occupied Arab territories and its refusal to implement the Geneva convention of 1949 on the protection of civilians in times of war, its policy of Judaizing the physical and cultural aspects of the occupied territories and considers that such acts and behaviour are war crimes and a challenge to mankind at large;

8. Considers that all the measures adopted by Israel in the occupied Arab territories and designed to alter their demographic, geographical, social, cultural and economic aspects—including those aiming at Judaizing the Holy City of Jerusalem are null and void and that under no circumstances can these measures or their consequences be recognized;

9. Condemns all States that provide military, economic and human support to Israel, and calls upon them to desist from doing do forthwith;

10. Calls upon all countries that have not yet done so, to sever political, cultural and economic relations with Israel;

11. Calls upon all OAU member-States to take all appropriate measures to intensify pressure against Israel at the UN

and other Agencies, including the possibility of eventually depriving it of its status as a member of these Agencies;

12. Decides to inscribe the item of the 'Question of Palestine' on the Agenda of the 26th Session of the Council;

13. Requests the Secretary-General to submit a report on the developments of the question of Palestine to the next Session.

Reservations:
Ghana—Sierra-Leone—Senegal—Liberia
Against:
Zaire

Appendix E:
Mideast-Related Resolutions Approved by the 1978 Organization of African Unity Summit Conference Held in Khartoum (Sudan)

(8) The Arab Homeland

(a) The summit reaffirms its support for the Arab countries in the conflict and for the people of Palestine in their legitimate struggle for the recovery of their usurped rights and vigorously condemns the aggressive plots of the Zionists, their expansionist policy and rejection of the United Nations' resolutions;

(b) Strongly condemns the profane alliance between Zionism and the racialist regimes of South Africa and Zimbabwe and urges all the member governments to be vigilant against the dangers of such an alliance which seeks domination and expansionism at the expense of the Arab countries. It reaffirms the right of the Arab countries to resist, and of the Palestinian people to gain full permanent sovereignty over their possessions and their other natural resources in the Arab occupied lands, and the right of the Palestinian people to receive full compensation for the extraction and exploitation of these riches;

(c) Strongly condemns the determination of the Zionists to follow up their expansionist policy and build illegal settlements in the Arab occupied lands. It demands that an end be immediately put to the installation of such settlements and that all the existing settlements be removed;

(d) Consistently backs up the Palestinian people in their struggle for the recovery of their legitimate national rights and

Source: *Africa Research Bulletin* Political, Social, and Cultural Series (July 1978):4914.

considers the Palestine Liberation Organisation as the only legitimate representative of the Palestinian people.

(9) The Palestinian Cause

(a) The summit reaffirms its support for the Palestinian people in their legitimate struggle by all possible means including the military struggle to regain their usurped rights. It also denounces the Zionist expansionist policy against the Palestinian people which reached its climax in the occupation of southern Lebanon last March;

(b) Urges the international community to increase the Zionists' isolation in the diplomatic, economic, political and military fields in compliance with the UN Charter. It further calls on the countries which have not yet recognised the rights of the Palestinian people to affirm these rights and it also calls for the recognition of the PLO as the sole legitimate representative of the Palestinian people.

Appendix F:
"The Cairo Declaration"—Political Declaration Endorsed by the First Afro-Arab Summit Conference Held in Cairo (Egypt) March 7-9, 1977

(1) The first conference of the heads of states and governments of the OAU and the Arab League met in Cairo from March 7th to 9th, 1977.

(2) The African and Arab heads of states and governments, guided by their peoples' faith in consolidating Arab-African co-operation—as based on the principles and aims contained in the OAU and the Arab League Charters—and by their common political desire, which they have expressed in numerous resolutions issued in this connection at the African and Arab summit conferences of the two organisations, have discussed and approved the draft declaration and the action programme prepared by the joint ministerial council held in Dakar from the April 19th to 22nd, 1976, concerning co-operation in the political, diplomatic, economic, trade, educational, cultural, scientific, social and technical fields.

(3) The Arab-African summit conference reaffirms its commitment to the principles of non-alignment and peaceful co-existence and to the establishment of a just international economic system.

(4) The Arab-African summit conference affirms its adherence to the principles of respecting sovereignty and territorial integrity, non-interference in the domestic affairs of other states, shunning aggression, the right to self-determination, the illegality of the forcible occupation and annexation of

Source: Africa Research Bulletin Political, Social, and Cultural Series (March 1977):4346-47.

territory, and the resolving of disputes and conflicts by peaceful means.

(5) The heads of African and Arab states and governments emphasise the need for strengthening the unified front of their peoples in their struggle for national liberation. They condemn imperialism, colonialism, neocolonialism, Zionism, racial segregation and all other forms of racial and sectarian discrimination, particularly its aspects as they are clear in southern Africa, Palestine and in the other Arab and African occupied territories. In this respect, they express their full support for the struggle of the peoples of Palestine, Zimbabwe, Namibia, South Africa and Djibouti—called the Somali Coast by the French—to recover their legitimate national rights and exercise their right to self-determination. They affirm their support for the political and regional unity of the Comoro Islands.

(6) The Arab-African summit conference calls on the OAU and the Arab League to exchange information in a regular manner on the development of the joint struggle of their peoples for liberation in Africa and the Middle East so that the member states will be able to perform an effective and positive role in this field.

(7) The heads of the African and Arab states and governments condemn the continuing military aggressions and all the political and economic manoeuvres which imperialism is practising through the racialist regimes in South Africa and Rhodesia and their allies against sovereign states, namely Angola, Botswana, Lesotho, Mozambique and Zambia to shake the political stability of their governments and undermine their efforts to achieve economic development. The summit conference considers these aggressions as being directed against the African and Arab world and that they constitute a threat to world peace. The conference also repudiates similar actions by Israel against Egypt, Jordan, Lebanon and Syria. The heads of the African and Arab states and governments have decided their countries should extend and increase their countries' material support and any other type of necessary aid to enable these countries to strengthen and defend their independence. The conference condemns the Israeli authorities for persisting in

changing the demographic and geographical conditions in the occupied Arab territories and for their violation of inter-, national law and UN resolutions. The conference demands that Israel should stop adopting these measures in order to create better conditions which would help a settlement in the area.

(8) The Arab-African summit conference resolves to continue to exert more efforts within the framework of the OAU, the Arab League, the United Nations and all other international platforms in the search for the most effective way to consolidate the political and economic isolation of Israel, South Africa and Rhodesia on the international level as long as those countries persist in their racialist, expansionist and aggressive policies. To achieve this, the summit conference stresses the imposing of complete political, diplomatic, cultural, sports and economic—particularly oil—bans against those regimes.

(9) The Arab-African summit conference expresses its complete conviction that the implementation of the declaration and the action programme related to African-Arab cooperation will be an historic turning point in strengthening all the bonds between the African and Arab States, consolidating their political independence and sovereignty, particularly their permanent sovereignty over their natural resources, strengthening the struggle of the peoples of the Third World and guaranteeing world peace and security.

(10) After a comprehensive study of the situation, the Arab-African summit conference expresses its deep concern regarding the problems of Palestine, the Middle East, Zimbabwe, Namibia and South Africa; it also expresses its full conviction that these are African-Arab issues. The conference resolves to extend its full support to the peoples struggling against racialist and Zionist regimes and to the front-line states neighbouring the confrontation areas to help them in their national liberation struggle.

(11) The summit conference strongly deplores the use of mercenaries and pledges to destroy this phenomenon.

(12) The Arab-African summit conference resolves to adopt all necessary measures to strengthen direct economic and trade

relations and dealings in all fields, particularly in the fields of trade, culture, education, science and art, between the African and Arab states.

(13) The heads of the African and Arab states and governments declare their firm faith in African-Arab co-operation. They announce their determination to mobilise all resources and exert all efforts to achieve the aims of the declaration and action programme of African-Arab co-operation in order to achieve more understanding among their peoples and establish African-Arab ties of fraternity on firm and lasting foundations.

Appendix G:
Arab Financial Institutions Providing Assistance for Economic Development

Multilateral Agencies

Name	Established	Capital	Type Funding	Recipients	Stated Purpose(s)
Arab Fund for Economic and Social Development (AFESD)	1968	$347m	Long-term loans	Arab League states	Private and public investments, two or more countries
Fund for Arab-African Technical Assistance (ATAFA or FAATA)	1973	$25m	Investment loans	African and Arab states	Promote technical cooperation
Arab Bank for Economic Development in Africa (BADEA)	1973(5)	$231m	Long-term soft loans	Non-Arab African states	Promote economic development, public investment
Islamic Development Bank (IDB)	1974	$2.4b	Interest-free loans	Arab states; non-Arab states (with Muslim majorities)	Economic and social development
OAPEC Special Account	1974	$80m	Interest-free loans with 75% grant element	Non-oil-producing Arab states	Emergency financial assistance
Special (Arab) Fund for Africa (SAFA)	1974	$200m	Loans at 1% p.a.	African MSA states	Compensation for losses due to higher oil prices
Arab Monetary Fund (AMF)	1977	$875m	Financial transfers	Arab subscribers	Balance-of-payments assistance

Bilateral Agencies

Name	Established	Capital	Type Funding	Recipients	Stated Purpose(s)
Kuwait Fund for Arab Economic Development (KFAED)	1961	$3.4b	Long-term soft loans	Originally only Arab states; after '74, some non-Arab LDCs	Economic development

Institution	Year	Amount	Type of loan	Recipients	Purpose
Abu Dhabi Fund for Arab Economic Development (ADFAED)	1971	$500m	Long-term soft loans	Originally only Arab states; after '75, some non-Arab LDCs	Economic development
Saudi Development Fund (SDF)	1974	$2.8b	Soft loans	Arab and non-Arab LDCs	Economic development; financial assistance
External Iraqi Fund for Development (EIFD)	1974	$500m	Soft loans	Arab and non-Arab LDCs	Economic assistance
Others					
Afro-Arab Bank of Cairo (AAB)	1964	$50m	Loans	Arab and African states	Economic development projects; external trade operations
Libyan Arab Foreign Bank (LAFB)	1972	$68m	"	Not specified	"
Union des Banques Arabo-Françaises (UBAF)	1970	FF110m	"	Mainly Arab states	"
International Arab Bank for External Trade and Development (IABETD)	1973	$75m	"	"	"
Kuwaiti-Senegalese Investment Bank (KSIB)	1974	$4m	"	Senegal	"
Kuwaiti Investment Co. (KIC)	1961	$25m	"	Not specified	Investment brokerage, management, underwriting
Kuwait Foreign Trading, Contracting and Investment Company	1965	$100m	"	Arab and African states	Banking investments, capital projects financing, "Afro-Arab cooperation"

Sources: Arab Economist, 4/77:38-43; Arab League Secretariat, Cairo.

Notes

1. Since almost all the news media in Africa are either government-controlled or reflect current official views, articles or news items about the Arab connection with slavery are almost always indications of African displeasure with the Arab link. Sometimes such items are quite blunt on the subject. For example, Albert Mvula, in a full-page, illustrated feature entitled "The Arabs, How Friendly?" in the *Zambia Daily Mail* (June 21, 1974), has this to say: "The refusal of the Arabs to sell oil to the African states at a reduced price is a tacit example that Arabs, our former slave masters, are not prepared to abandon the rider and horse partnership. We have not forgotten that they used to drive us like herds of cattle and sell us as slaves." The Swahili-language *Uhuru* (Dar es Salaam, Tanzania, May 5, 1973), on the occasion of a suggestion by Colonel Qaddhafi that the OAU headquarters be moved to Libya, printed an "Open Letter to Qadhafi," which included the following: "Tanzania remembers the slave trade practised by Arabs. We regret the way you mistreated our forefathers in slavery, and we know how badly people with African blood are mistreated in your countries like Muscat and Oman, where they were sent as slaves." For additional examples of African comments on the subject, see the *Daily Nation* (Nairobi, January 10, 1972) article titled, "Kenyans used as slaves in Yemen, says Cotu"; a long, illustrated piece on "To the Roots of Slavery" by Wade Hui in the *Nation* (September 8, 1977) noting recent scholarship on Arab slaving in East Africa; as well as the *New York Times* of June 20, 1974, citing Archbishop Yago of Abidjan and the

Washington Post on March 3, 1975, quoting the Ethiopian *Herald*'s chief columist.

2. Joseph Cuoq (1977:6,7) reports that in 1974 some 346, 711 African pilgrims were registered in Mecca, of which 138,937 came from countries other than those of the Maghreb, Libya, and Egypt. Nigeria alone accounted for 51,764. Cuoq also reports that in 1973-74, of the 31,680 students at al-Azhar, over 4,000 were foreigners (i.e., non-Egyptians), of which latter number about 1,000 came from sub-Saharan Africa.

3. Eight African countries broke relations with Israel before the war: Uganda (March 1972), Chad (November 1972), Congo People's Republic (December 1972), Niger and Mali (January 1973), Burundi (May 1973), Togo (September 1973), and Zaire (October 1973). After the outbreak of fighting, the rest—with the exceptions noted—followed suit. Guinea broke relations with Israel in 1967.

4. The November 1973 Conference of Arab Heads of State in Algiers adopted a declaration rendering "vibrant homage to their brother states in Africa" for having manifested "solidarity with the just cause of the Arab peoples, whose struggle is included in the fight of all liberation forces against colonialism, racism, imperialism, and Zionism," and unanimously and solemnly "reaffirmed that 'Afro-Arab solidarity' should express itself concretely in all domains and in particular in those of political and economic cooperation, so as to reinforce the independent states and promote development" (League of Arab States, Information Section; Cairo, 1973). Similar resolutions were adopted by the OAU ministerial and general meetings in 1974, and were echoed by the OAU each year from 1975 to 1978.

5. Another widely held misconception is that the 1973 "oil crisis" was precipitated, if not caused, by the Arab-Israeli conflict. This is not only categorically wrong but tends to spread self-serving assertions about the connection. The facts are that the October 1973 war apparently provided OPEC with the opportunity to accomplish rapidly what it had hoped to do gradually. Following a decade of stable oil prices, OPEC raised prices sharply during the three years preceding the October war, that is, between the Tehran agreement of February 1971

and October 1, 1973, the market price of oil was raised by 123 percent. The embargo, to be sure, involved sizable production cutbacks, particularly by Saudi Arabia, the largest producer and the one that could most easily absorb whatever losses were incurred thereby. The Saudis did effect cutbacks, but hardly suffered: their production for the whole of 1973 was 26 percent above that of 1972, and during the embargo period—October 1973 through March 1974—they still managed to produce some 6 percent more than during the corresponding period 1972-73. Moreover, given the increases in price announced in December 1973—to take effect on January 1, 1974—of 130 percent above that announced on October 16, 1973, they and their OPEC partners only gained, not lost, on the entire exercise. As if to underline the absence of a political connection between the "oil crisis" and the October war, the embargo itself was lifted in March 1974 without any of the announced conditions for its termination (i.e., implementation of UN Resolution 242 on standard Arab terms—withdrawal from occupied territories, satisfaction of Palestinian demands, etc.) having been met. During the 1971-73 period in question the posted price was raised by 67 percent, but the government "take" per barrel rose by 121 percent on the basis of self-implementing increases called for in ARAMCO's participation agreements. We are indebted to Benjamin Schwadran for some of the insights in this note.

6. Dector (1977) notes that twenty-seven African states currently trade with Israel, that the 1975 Africa-Israel trade of these states came to $66.4 million, an increase of 16 percent over 1974. Israel does not publish details of its trade with African states with which it has no diplomatic relations. However, we were informed by senior Israeli officials in Jerusalem that not only had the trend noted by Dector continued through 1976 and 1977, but that trade was worth approximately $100 millions per annum, excluding retransfers and accounting *only* for exports to Black African countries. We were also informed that the number of Israelis in Black Africa—outside the four African countries that still recognize Israel—has grown considerably during the period in question. Almost all these Israelis are attached to Israeli companies doing business in Africa; the

largest numbers appear to be in the Ivory Coast, Nigeria, Kenya, Zaire, and Malawi. Israel also imports some of its oil from Gabon. All this permitted a senior Israeli official to undertake, early in 1978, a nine-country tour to African states south of the Sahara and north of the Zambezi. By his own account, he was extremely well received and was told more than once that, were it not for Arab pressure, a good many African states would prefer to resume open diplomatic and trade relations with Israel. (The official in question asked that he not be identified.)

7. The terms "banker" and "industrializer" are used here without further explanation in order to maintain the flow of the argument. The distinctions between these categories are discussed in Chapter 6.

8. Iran is not, of course, an Arab state. It is, however, Muslim and a charter member of OPEC, and since its former leaders chose to follow the new Arab-dominated developmental thrust, it is included in this analysis.

9. The Al Maaref edition, also Cairo 1954, contains the following additional sentence: "There remains an important question, that of the Nile, the vital artery of our homeland whose sources are in the center of Africa."

10. The Al Maaref edition translates this sentence (from the original Arabic) as follows: "Equally, there is also the [question of the] Sudan, whose frontiers extend to Africa's central regions."

References

Abiaka, I. 1974. The Energy Crisis and the LDCs. *Columbia Journal of World Business* 9, no. 3 (Fall):318-36.

Africa Confidential. 1972. 13 (October):5.

Africa Currents. 1976-78.

African Development. 1975-78.

Afro-Asian Affairs. 1975. Economic and Petroleum News. 17 (September).

Afro-Asian News. 1975. Special Report: The Impact of the High Price of Oil on the African Consumer Countries. No. 17 (October).

Akinsanya, A. 1976. The Afro-Arab Alliance: Dream or Reality. *African Affairs* 75, no. 30 (October):511-29.

Aluko, O. 1976. Oil at Concessionary Prices for Africa: A Case-Study in Nigerian Decision-Making. *African Affairs* 75, no. 30 (October):425-43.

Amir, S. 1974. *Israel's Development Cooperation.* New York: Praeger.

Arab Bank for Development in Africa. 1976. *Newsletter* 1 (January).

Arab Economist. 1975-78.

ARB/EFT—*Africa Research Bulletin.* Economic, Financial, and Technical Series. 1972-78.

ARB/PSC—*Africa Research Bulletin.* Political, Social, and Cultural Series. 1973-78.

Asfahany, N. 1977. *Afro-Arab Cooperation: Political and Financial Developments.* Rome: Instituto Affari Internazionali.

Awdah, Abd Al-Malik. 1975. African Attitudes Towards the Arabs. *Al-Siyāseh Al-Dawlīyah*. Cairo. (February). Trans. by E. Sivan.

Bamisaye, A. 1974. The Politics of Oil. Unpub. paper: African Studies Association, Brandeis University, Waltham, Massachusetts.

Banker. 1977. Oil and Money in the Middle East: A Survey. 127, no. 613 (March).

Barnet, J., and E. Mueller. 1974. *Global Reach: The Power of the Multinational Corporations*. New York: Simon and Schuster.

Baulin, J. 1962. *The Arab Role in Africa*. Baltimore: Penguin Books.

BE—Bank of England. 1978. *Quarterly Bulletin* 18, no. 1 (March):29.

Beim, D. O. 1977. Rescuing the LDCs. *Foreign Affairs* 55, no. 4 (July):717-31.

Bell, J. B. 1973. *The Horn of Africa: Strategic Magnet in the Seventies*. New York: Crane and Russak.

BIS—Bank for International Settlements. 1976. *Forty-Sixth Annual Report*. Basle: BIS.

Bissell, R. 1976. Africa and the Nations of the Middle East. *Current History* 71, no. 421 (November):158-60, 181-82.

Blair, J. M. 1976. *The Control of Oil*. New York: Pantheon Books.

Bobrow, D.; R. Kurdle; and D. Pirages. 1977. Contrived Scarcity: The Short-Term Consequences of Expensive Oil. *International Studies Quarterly* 21, no. 4 (December): 619-45.

Bouvier, P. 1974. L'Afrique à l'heure algérienne: Les Chances du rapprochement Arabo-Africain. *Studia Diplomatica* 28, no. 3:305-25.

Business Week. 1975-77.

Bustros, G. 1978. The Burning Question. *Africa* 77 (January): 91-98.

Chibwe, E. 1976. *Arab Dollars for Africa*. London: Croon and Helm.

Cleveland, H. Van B., and W. H. B. Brittain. 1977. Are the LDCs in Over Their Heads? *Foreign Affairs* 55, no. 4 (July):732-50.

Cremeans, C. 1973. *The Arabs and the World: Nasser's Arab Nationalist Policy.* New York: Praeger.

Cuoq, J. M. 1975. *Les Musulmans en Afrique.* Paris: Maisonneuve et Larose.

————. 1977. Le Monde Arabo-Islamique et l'Afrique. *Afrique Contemporaine* 90 (March-April):1-8.

Decalo, S. 1967. Africa and the Mid-Eastern war. *Africa Report* 7, no. 12 (October):57-61.

Dector, M. 1977. Black Africa's Trade with Israel Thrives and Grows. New York: Media Project, Black-Jewish Information Center.

Development Forum. 1978.

Drysdale, J. 1964. *The Somalia Dispute.* London: Pall Mall.

Erb, G. F., and V. Kallab. 1975. *Beyond Dependency: The Developing World Speaks Out.* Washington, D.C.: Overseas Development Council.

Erb, G. F., and H. C. Low. 1977. Resource Transfers to the Developing World. In *Oil, the Arab-Israeli Dispute, and the Industrial World,* edited by J. C. Hurewitz, pp. 212-30. Boulder, Colo.: Westview.

Financial Times. 1975. Arab Countries Spread the Oil Fortunes. (April 21):22.

Froelich, J. C. 1965a. La progression de l'Islam et de la culture arabe au Sud de Sahara. *Le Mois en Afrique* 1 (November).

————. 1965b. Les rapports de l'Afrique noire avec le monde arabe et les chances du pan-africanisme. *Revue de Psychologie des Peuples* (Le Havre) 2 (4th quarter):455-65.

————.1968. Relationships between Islam and Africa North and South of the Sahara. *Africa Forum* 2 and 3 (Fall and Winter):44-57.

Galtung, J. 1976. The Lomé Convention and Neo-Capitalism. *African Review* 6, no. 1:33-41.

Gerschenkron, A. 1962, *Economic Backwardness in Historical Perspective.* Cambridge, Mass.: Harvard University Press.

————. 1968. *Continuity in History and Other Essays.* Cambridge, Mass.: Harvard University Press.

————. 1970. *Europe in the Russian Mirror: Four Lectures in Economic History.* London: Cambridge University Press.

Gitelson, A. 1974. Why Do Small States Break Diplomatic

Relations with Outside Powers? Lessons from the African Experience. *International Studies Quarterly* 18, no. 4 (December):451-84.

———. 1976. Israel's African Setback in Perspective. In *Israel in the Third World,* edited by Michael A. Curtis and Susan A. Gitelson, pp. 182-99. New Brunswick: Transaction Books.

Green, R. H. 1976. The Lomé Convention: Updated Dependence or Departure Toward Collective Self-Reliance? *African Review* 6, no. 1:44-53.

Hahn, L. 1975. *Arabs and Africans: Cooperation and Conflict.* Middle East Problems Paper 14. Washington, D.C. Middle East Institute.

Hameed, K. A. 1976. The Oil Revolution and African Development. *African Affairs* 75, no. 300 (July):349-58.

Hodges, T. 1978. Western Sahara; The Escalating Confrontation. *Africa Report* 23, no. 2 (March-April)4-9.

Horowitz, I. 1965. *Three Worlds of Development: The Theory and Practice of International Stratification.* London: Oxford University Press.

IBRD—International Bank for Reconstruction and Development (World Bank). 1976. *Energy and Petroleum in Non-OPEC Developing Countries, 1974-1980.* Staff Working Paper no. 229. New York: IBRD.

———. 1977. *Tanzania Basic Economic Report, Main Report.* New York: IBRD.

IMF/IFS—International Monetary Fund. *International Financial Statistics.* 1976, 1977, 1978.

Interdependent. 1976. Petrodollars and Apartheid. 3, no. 2:1, 4.

Ismael, T. Y. 1968. Religion and UAR Policy. *Journal of Modern African Studies* 6, no. 1 (May):49-57.

———. 1971. *The U.A.R. in Africa.* Evanston, Ill.: Northwestern University Press.

Jansen, G. H. 1966. *Non-alignment and the Afro-Asian States.* New York: Praeger.

Junqua, D. 1978. The Trap Springs on Mauritania. *Guardian* (March 5):12.

Kanovsky, E. 1977. *Recent Economic Developments in the Middle East.* Occasional Papers no. 54. Tel Aviv University: Shiloah Center.

Kenen, P. 1975. In *Report of the Oxford Seminar on Oil Wealth, Discrimination, and Freedom of Trade* (July 7-9), pp. 29-31. Oxford: Christ Church College.

Kerekes, T., ed. 1961. *The Arab Middle East and Muslim Africa.* New York: Praeger.

Krapels, E. N. 1977. *Oil and Security: Problems and Prospects of Importing Countries.* Adelphi Papers 136. London: International Institute for Strategic Studies.

Kreinin, M. E. 1964. *Israel and Africa: A Study in Technical Cooperation.* New York: Praeger.

Legum, C. 1965. *Pan-Africanism.* New York: Praeger.

_____. 1976. Africa, Arabs, and the Middle East. In *Africa Contemporary Record Annual Survey and Documents 1975-76,* edited by C. Legum, pp. A76-A87. New York: Africana.

_____. 1977. The Afro-Arab Summit, 1977. In *African Contemporary Record Annual Survey and Documents 1976-77,* edited by C. Legum, pp. A96-A107. New York: Africana.

Le Monde. 1978. Points de vue sur l'intervention française du Tchad. (June 13):4.

Lewis, B. 1976. The Anti-Zionist Resolution. *Foreign Affairs* 55, no. 1 (October):54-64.

Los Angeles Times. 1975. (August 31):5.

Lottem, E. 1977. Arab Aid to Africa. Paper for Conference on Middle East and Africa, May 31, 1977, at Harry S. Truman Research Institute, Hebrew University, Jerusalem.

Low, H. C. 1974. The Oil-Dependent Developing Countries. *Current History* 69, no. 407 (July-Aug.):19-24, 46.

Mazrui, A. A. 1975a. Black Africa and the Arabs. *Foreign Affairs* 53, no. 4 (July):725-42.

_____. 1975b. Afro-Arab Relations and the Role of the Gulf States of Eastern Arabia. *Pan-Africanist* 6 (June):30-32.

MEED—*Middle East Economic Digest.* 1975-78.

_____. 1976. *Special Report on Saudi Arabia* (December).

Middle East Economic Survey. 1975-76.

Mikdashi, Z. 1975. The OPEC Process. *Daedalus* 104, no. 4 (Fall):205-6.

Morgan Guaranty Trust Co. 1976. *World Financial Markets* (September).

Mortimer, E. 1978. Western Sahara: The Diplomatic Perspectives. *Africa Report* 23, no. 2 (March-April):10-14.

Mushkat, M. 1971. Die israelish-Afrikanische Zusammenarbeit. *Intenationales Afrikaforum* 12:465-72.

Mwamba, Z. 1973. Egypt's Contribution to African Liberation. Unpub. paper: African Studies Association, Brandeis University, Waltham, Massachusetts.

Nasser, G. A. 1954. *Philosophy of the Revolution*, pp. 68-70. Cairo: National Publishing House.

National Journal. 1976. When the Run on the Bank Heads Toward the U.S. and the IMF. 8, no. 5 (December):1722-79.

Neuberger, B. 1975. Racial Nationalism in Black Africa. *Weiner Library Bulletin* 28:35-36, 50-56.

New York Times. 1977. (January 30):11.

_____. 1978. (May 12, 13).

Oded, A. 1974. Slaves and Oil: The Arab Image in Black Africa. *Weiner Library Bulletin* 27:34-47.

OECD—Organization for Economic Cooperation and Development. 1975. *1975 Review of Development Cooperation Efforts and Policies of the Development Assistance Committee.* Paris: OECD.

_____. (1976). *Review of Development Cooperation Efforts and Policies of the Development Assistance Committee.* Paris: OECD.

Oppenheim, V. H. 1976. Arab Tankers Move Downstream. *Foreign Policy* 23 (Summer):117-30.

Petroleum Intelligence Weekly. 1976 (March 15).

Raphael, A. 1975. Arab Oil Wealth Starts to Flow in Africa. *African Development* 9, no. 25 (May):24-27.

Remba, O. 1976. Arab Oil and America's Energy Dilemmas. *Midstream* 22, no. 6:28-41.

Renninger, J. P. 1976. After the Seventh Special General Assembly Session: Africa and the New Emerging World. *African Studies Review* 19, no. 2 (September):35-48.

Rivlin, B., and J. Fomerand. 1976. Changing Third World Perspectives and Policies Toward Israel. In *Israel in the Third World,* edited by Michael Curtis and Susan A. Gitelson, pp. 325-60. New Brunswick: Transaction Books.

Rondot, P. 1977. Monde arabe et Afrique: relations politiques. *Afrique Contemporaine* 90 (March-April):10-15.

Sharshar, A. M. 1977. Oil, Religion, and Mercantilism: A Study of Saudi Arabia's Economic System. *Studies in Comparative International Development* 12, no. 3 (Fall):46-64.

Sheehan, E. R. F. 1976. The Epidemic of Money. *New York Times Magazine* (November 14):36, 112-18.

Sirkin, R. M. 1975. Israeli-African Relations: The Fall From Grace. Unpub. paper: African Studies Association, Brandeis University, Waltham, Mass.

Thompson, W. S. 1969. *Ghana's Foreign Policy*. Princeton, N.J.: Princeton University Press.

Tibi, E. 1971. Aegypten in Afrika. *Afrika Heute* 16 (August): 343-45.

Timmler, M. 1974. Getäuschte oder enttäuschte Afrikaner. *Aussenpolitik* 25:329-40.

Tucker, R. W. 1977. Oil and American Power: Three Years Later. *Commentary* 63, no. 1 (January):18-29.

UNCTAD—United Nations Conference on Trade and Development. 1976. *Handbook of International Trade and Development Statistics*. New York: UNCTAD.

————. 1977. *Interdependence of Problems of Trade, Development Finance, and the International Monetary System*. Doc. no. TD/B/665 Add. 1, Parts 1 and 2 (July 25). Geneva: UNCTAD.

U.S. Congress, Senate, Subcommittee on Foreign Assistance of the Committee on Foreign Relations. 1976. *IDB and AFDF Authorization: Hearing on H.R. 9721*. 94th cong., 1st sess., 28 January 1976.

————. 1977. *African Development Fund: Hearing on H.R. 5262*. 95th Cong., 1st sess., 18 April 1977.

Vermont, R. 1972. Le Moyen-Orient et l'Afrique. *Revue de Défense Nationale* (January):79-93.

Von Schack, A. 1977. Black Africa and Its Arab Neighbours to the North. *Aussenpolitik* 28, no. 1 (First Quarter):110-15.

Wariavwalla, B. 1975. The Energy Crisis, the Developing World, and Strategy. In *Adelphi Papers 115*, pp. 32-37. London: International Institute for Strategic Studies.

West Africa. 1966 and 1973-78.

West, R. L. 1974. Trade versus Aid Revisited: Petro-Deficits and the Pattern of African Terms-of-Trade. Unpub. paper: Fletcher School of Law and Diplomacy, Tufts University, Medford, Mass.

Woronoff, J. 1970. *Organizing African Unity*. Metuchen, N.J.: Scarecrow Press.

Wright, J. 1977. Africa, Prospects for New Oil Discoveries. *Petroleum Economist* 44, no. 2 (February):45-47.

Yaori, S. 1974. The Oil Crisis: The Plight of the Developing Countries. Unpub. manuscript: School of Petroleum Studies, Tel Aviv University.

Zartman, I. W. 1966. *International Relations in the New Africa*. Englewood Cliffs, N.J.: Prentice-Hall.

Index